A
PRACTICAL GUIDE
TO
LIBRARY MANAGEMENT

Table of Contents

A Practical Guide To Library Management......................................1

PREFACE......................................3

CHAPTER 1......................................8

CHAPTER 2......................................11

CHAPTER 3......................................15

CHAPTER 4......................................17

CHAPTER 5......................................20

CHAPTER 6......................................25

CHAPTER 7......................................32

CHAPTER 8......................................36

CHAPTER 9......................................38

CHAPTER 10......................................42

CHAPTER 11......................................44

CHAPTER 12......................................54

CHAPTER 13......................................56

CHAPTER 14......................................60

CHAPTER 15......................................67

CHAPTER 16......................................69

CHAPTER 17......................................71

CHAPTER 18......................................74

CHAPTER 19......................................77

CHAPTER 20......................................80

CHAPTER 21......................................87

CHAPTER 22......................................88

CHAPTER 23......................................94

CHAPTER 24......................................96

CHAPTER 25......................................101

CHAPTER 26......................................105

CHAPTER 27......................................111

CHAPTER 28......................................114

CHAPTER 29......................................118

CHAPTER 30.. 122
CHAPTER 31.. 123
CHAPTER 32.. 125
CHAPTER 33.. 129
CHAPTER 34.. 132
CHAPTER 35.. 134
CHAPTER 36.. 136
CHAPTER 37.. 138
CHAPTER 38.. 144
CHAPTER 39.. 146
CHAPTER 40.. 147

Authors

DR. KAUSHAL KISHOR CHAUDHARY

M.COM, MLISc., DIT, LL.B, Ph.D.

&

RAM NIVAS KUMAR

M.A. (English), MJMC, MLISc., Dip-In-OA

Edition
2024
Copyright
Ram Nivas Kumar
Publishing right
Ram Nivas Kumar
First published in 2019

PREFACE

Library management is not a new concept. Evolved with the inception of the library, its original concept that lacked systematic procedure and scientific application have undergone a remarkable change. In this circumstance, we need such a book that it may meet the new requirements of the students and the professionals of Library Science.

After having gone through several books on Library Science and made an in-depth study, it cropped me up high that I must write a book on library management to fulfil the above requirements. Also, some college students of Library Science have been asking me to write on the subject for a long. Though lots of books are available on the subject, yet there is not such a single book that may contain all issues relating to the library management. In this situation, it becomes tough for the students to read so many books onone subject. Hence, Idecided to write such a book that may contain all essential issues in brief to facilitate the students and other readers.

Keeping this literary idea in view, I approached to a well-known Library Science scholar Dr. Kaushal Kishor Chaudhary, Deputy Librarian, Central Library, BRA Bihar University, Muzaffarpur and requested him for his valuable suggestions and literary assistance which heacceded to gladly and supplied me with his important contents on several chapters. This book is the outcome of this idea and subsequent efforts thereupon.

A Practical Guide to Library Management is intended to serve the important need of the present-day learners and professionals of library management. An attempt has been made in this book to give in brief the learning on almost all issues of good library management. In a nutshell, the book has been made broad-based in order to serve the needs of a wider section of students.It is not only hoped but is my firm belief that it would be helpful to improve the achievement level of students of Library and Information Science.

We are grateful to Prof. Mahendra Pratap Singh, Head of the Department, Library and Information Science, BBA Central University, Lucknow for his valuable suggestions and academic support on the writing of this book. We are indebted to Prof. Hirak Kanti Chakraborty, Head of the Department, Library and Information Science, S N S University, Varanasi for hisencouragement, motivation and assistance with highlevel learning material on the subject. We are highly grateful to Dr. Deepak Kumar, an Income Tax Officerand litterateur for going through the entire manuscript and doing overall editing work of the book.

We have taken utmost care while publishing this book. However, to err is human. Inadvertent errors, if any, may please be brought to our notice. Comments and suggestions are mostwelcome.

-Ram Nivas Kumar

CONTENTS

1. Meaning of Library

2. Public Library System in India

3. Prominent Libraries in India

4. Prominent Libraries in the World

5. Role of Library

6. Academic Library: Objectives and Functions

7. College and University Library

8. National Library

9. Public Library: Importance and Functions

10. Library Profession

11. Five Laws of Library Science

12. Position and Functions of Librarian

13. Library Professionals Association

14. Ethics of the American Library Association

15. Financial Sources of Library

16. Library Legislation in India

17. Library Legislation: Necessity and Importance

18. Delivery of Books Act

19. Copyright Laws

20. Library Rules

21. Reprography

22. Essentials of Library Science

23. Library Display

24. Principles of Library Management

25. Library Cooperation

26. Library Public Relations

27. Library Extension Services

28. Functions of Acquisition Section

29. Accession Register

30. Library Book Number

31. International Standard Book Number

32. Cataloguing

33. Importance of Library Catalogue

34. Book Circulation

35. Reference Section

36. Periodical Section

37. Book Maintenance Section

38. Repair and Binding of Books

39. Stock Rectification

40. Stock Verification

References

CHAPTER 1

MEANING OF LIBRARY

The library is a collection of sources of information for reading and reference or borrowing. It provides physical or digital access to reading and learning material. According to Oxford Advanced Learner's Dictionary, "Library is a building in which collections of books, CDs, newspapers, etc. are kept for people toread, study or borrow.The dictionary further enumerates that it is a room in a large house where most of the books, personal collection, other reading material, CDs, etc. are kept."For example- a public library, a reference library, a university library, etc.The Hindi wordPustakalayaisgenerallyused for the term "Library." In Hindi, the word *pustakalaya* means the place where books are kept. This is the original meaning of the word "Library." It is also known as granthalaya, granthagar, kutubkhana or kitabghar. When we visit a library, we see things as under:

  i.   Huge stock of books.
  ii. Readers are reading the books.
  iii. Different types of works being performed by the various staff for the effective use of the books.

In this way, it can be said that the collectionof books for public use inthelibrary. We can also say that an organized collection of books, magazines and other readable and audio, video material is a library.

HISTORY OF LIBRARY:In ancient times, pieces of knowledge and information were written on earthen slabs, tree's bark (*Bhojptra*),copper leaf, etc. We can call them the ancestors of the modern library. Earlier to the invention of paper and printing,knowledge was recorded on these objects only. The arrival of books in human life has taken place earlier than the invention of paper and printing. In the beginning, the work of writing was performed for the fulfilment of under mentioned objectives:

i.   To keepapersonal account.
ii. To write general and remarkable matters.
iii. To have a record of Government orders.
iv. For the publicity of work.

By the end of the medieval period, libraries began to be established and owned for personal and family uses. The contemporary learned scholars and sages preserved ancient and traditional cultural treasure. Rich people maintained a rich collection of books for their prestige and dignity. Kings and emperors maintained libraries in their palaces for the sake of knowledge, dignity and love for books. They founded a library to serve the state and the church; to sing the glory of their founders and for expansion of scientific knowledge for common people.

Later on, the foundation of libraries was no more a personal cause but a public one. In other words, they began to be founded for the use of the public at large.

In the modern age, the invention of the press, its expansion and the rise of democratic ideologies contributed a lot to the increase in the public use of books. The number of printed books kept on increasing. The books began to be available for common readers. Consequently, the number of learned increased. New subjects began to be created.

During the 18th century Industrial Revolution, the people grew more conscious of their rights. The humanistic approach began to spread everywhere. The culture and civilization of other countries began to be presented publicly. Hence, the importance of the library increased.

It is always necessary to keep a record of every new thing. It began to be published and presented by various media. Books and their other forms became essential for the existence of improved civilization and culture, their publicity and expansion. In the 20th century, a fundamental change came in the form of a library. By the 20th century, in libraries, not only books but also microfilms, video, computer, TV, etc. began to be collected and preserved for the publicity and expansion of knowledge.

CHAPTER 2

PUBLIC LIBRARY SYSTEM IN INDIA

An important landmark in the history of public library services in India was made by Maharaja SayajiRaoGaekwad by introducing free compulsory elementary education backed by the library in 1883 in the district of Baroda, and thus free public library services in India were introduced as a system in 1907. It can, therefore, be traced out that 2007 is the centenary year of free public library services in India. In spite of several drawbacks, the public library system in India has made considerable progress.

A public library is regarded as the people's source of learning and wisdom. It caters to the sections of the public with information and knowledge. It supports individuals in life-long learning. Education and library are inter-related. The history of the development ofapublic library may be said to be as old as that of education in India. During ancient times, the seekers of education used to stay in the Ashrams of Gurus for several years. Students joined Ashrams from many neighbouring countries. The oral tradition of education was imported were writing was not available in early times. Writing tradition came a little bit later. This is evident from the written and recorded material found in India. In the Ashrams, the manuscripts were kept for the use of the teachers and students as well as for the visitors. Ashrams were known as Vidyapeeth, where numbers of teachers are engaged to teachstudents like modern universities.

References are available to prove that NalandaUniverity in Bihar had its own multi-storied library in 600 AD with a massive collection of manuscripts.The collection of the library was housed in three buildings, each having nine floors and three hundred rooms. This library was opened by the then Emperor of India, King Davapal. The library was opened for known scholars who took an interest in reading, interpreting and even copying the documents kept in the library. The

Chinese traveller Huen Tsang is known to have consulted this library in the seventh century and to have taken from here hundreds of treaties to China and Japan. This library was completely destroyed by a Turkish Muslim invader BakhtiyarKhilji in 1193 AD.

Libraries in ancient India also developed as other famous centres of learningsuch as Vikramshila and Odantapuriuniversities of ancient India. Taxila and Vikramshila also have valuable manuscripts and collection on *Tantras* in their libraries.

Medieval Period (1200-1757 AD): Muslims ruled India in the medieval period, and hence, it is also known as the Mughal period. All the succession of rulers, namely, Babur, Humayun, Akbar and Jahangir, etc. made their distinctive contributions to education and libraries. Babur established the first Mughal Imperial Library in 1526 and his son Humayun set up a library at the Agra Fort with books, portfolios, picture books and beautiful works of calligraphy. After the death of Humayun, Akbar improved the management of the library with the same technique works and appointed calligraphers to copy good manuscripts. He also established a separate library for women at FatehpurSikri. Jahangir, another ruler of Mughal period, made a law that when a wealthy man dies heirless, the property should be used for building and repairing schools, monasteries, libraries, and other institutions, which helped the development of libraries in the late medieval period. During this period, the library staff had distinct designations like Nizam (Head Librarian), and Muhatin (Assistant Librarian) and those were assisted by scribes, illustrators, calligraphers and copyists.

During the late medieval period, Christian missionaries also contributed to the development of education and libraries.

The British Period (1757-1947): Though the British came to India primarily to establish trade and commerce, they established a number of educational societies with libraries in India. The establishment of the Bengal Royal Asiatic Society Library (1784), the Bombay Royal Asiatic

Society (1804) and the Calcutta Public Library (1835) enlightened the public with knowledge. The important libraries set up in 19th century in India are Andrews Library, Surat (1850), Gaya Public Library (1855), Long Library, Rajkot (1856), Connemara Public Library, Madras (1860), Baroda State Library (1877), Cochin Public Library and Reading Room, Trichur (1873) , Indore General Library (1852), Maharaja's Public Library, Jaipur (1899), Jammu and Kashmir Library (1879). The Calcutta Public Library became Imperial Library in 1903 and later became the National Library of India after independence.

A very significant contribution to the public library movement in India was made by His Highness the Maharaja of BarodaSayajiRao III Gaekwad. He is remembered today as the "Father of Library Movement in India." As education is the foundation to reconstruct a new social and economic life, he introduced free and compulsory education in his princely states. Thus, Baroda became the first state among the native states in British India to have compulsory free primary education. He also decided to establish a library as an experiment in one of the towns with State financial assistance. In 1906, he went to America and studied the libraries there. He was very much impressed by the library services there for the development of the people in their social, economic and educational life.

Dr S. R. Ranganathan also placed a significant role in library development as well as knowledge of library science. After joining the post of University Librarian at the University of Madras in 1924, Dr Ranganathan went to the United Kingdom and joined the knowledge committee on libraries. Ranganathan published his *Five Laws of Library Science* (1931), *Colon Classification* (1933),and *Classified Catalogue Code* (1934).Healsoprepared a *ModelPublic* Library *Bill* which helped to enact Public Library Legislation in the Indian States. Dr Ranganathan has made a noteworthy contribution to the domain knowledge of library science through his 60 books and 2000 seminal research articles during his lifetime and has been revered as the "Father of Library Science in India."

Post Independence Period: Public libraries in India made tremendous growth after independence. The Union and the State Government took considerable interest in the development of education and considered the library as an essential part of it. To enhance the level of literacy, the government initiated some programmes such as extension service, continuing education, social education, non-formal education and adult education. The public libraries played a considerable role in the community. The Delhi Public Library was established in 1951 under the joint auspices of the UNESCO and the Government of India to serve as a model Public Library for Asia.

In 1954, the Delivery of Books Act was passed and later amended in 1956 to include newspapers also. As per the Act, every publisher in India is obliged to deposit one copy each of its publications to the National Library in Calcutta, the Asiatic Society Library in Bombay, and the Connemara Public Library in Madras and the Delhi Public Library in New Delhi.

Rajaram Mohan Roy Library Foundation: It is an autonomous body under the Department of Cultureestablished in 1972 with the main objective to promote and support public library movement in the country. Grants are provided toother libraries by the Foundation to assist their services in development.

In 1979, a separate Library Section was established in the Department of Culture under the Ministry of Education, Government of India with an objective to promote and develop public libraries in India.

CHAPTER 3

PROMINENT LIBRARIES IN INDIA

NATIONAL LIBRARY, CALCUTTA: The National Library of India is located at Belvedere, Kolkata, West Bengal. It has a history of nearly two centuries. It was originally established in 1835 as Calcutta Public Library and was running on a proprietary basis. The Governor-General Lord Metcalf transferred 41, 675 Volumes from the library of the College of Fort William to the Calcutta Public Library. In addition to these books, the donation of books from individuals formed the nucleus of the library. Prince Dwarkanath Tagore was the first proprietor of the Calcutta Public Library.

After the independence, the Government changed the name of the Imperial Library as the National Library by an enactment of the Imperial Library (Change of Name) Act, 1948 and the collection was shifted from the Esplanade to the present Belvedere Estate. On 1st February 1953, the National Library was opened to the public. The library is under the Department of Culture, Ministry of Tourism,Government of India.

KHUDA BAKHSH ORIENTAL PUBLIC LIBRARY, PATNA: The KhudaBakhsh Oriental Public Library, Patna had its origin in the personal collection of a bibliophile,MaulviKhudaBakhsh, who donated his entire collection of 4,000 oriental manuscripts to the nation by a Deed of Trust. It was open for the public in October 1891, by Sir Charles Elliot, Governor of Bengal. Acknowledging the immense historical and intellectual value of its rich and valued collection, the Government of India settled the library as an Institution of national importance by an Act of Parliament- KhudaBakhsh Oriental Public Library Act, 1969. The library is now fully funded by the Ministry of Culture, Government of India. A Board governs this autonomous institution with the Governor of Bihar as its ex-officio

Chairman. The library has a rich collection of Mughal paintings, calligraphy and board decorations, besides manuscripts in Arabic and Urdu languages.

RAMPUR RAZA LIBRARY, RAMPUR: Rampur Raza Library, Rampur (Uttar Pradesh) had its origin in the personal collection of NawabFaizullah Khan who ruled the State of Rampur from 1774 to 1794. He established the library with his personal collection kept in the ToshaKhana of his palace. The Government of India took over the library on 1 July 1975 under the Act of Parliament and declared it as an institution of national importance. The library is under the Department of Culture, Government of India. It containsarare and valuable collection of manuscripts, historical documents, a specimen of Islamic calligraphy, miniature, paintings, astronomical instrument and illustrated works in Arabic and Persian languages with 80,000 printed books.

Aims and Objectives of Library Movement: Library movement aims to disseminate knowledge among the people for better living. The old idea that a public library is a mere storehouse of books and the librarian is its custodian only became outdated. The library movement conceived that a public library is a People's University.

The library movement aimed at achieving the overall development of human personality and to realize the objective of the library as an effective means. The movement wished to spread knowledge among the people and awoke the "Atma" of the individual from steep ignorance and inertia and help him in leading a fruitful and purposeful life in society. The main purpose of a public library is to help a reader to use documents for enriching his knowledge at leisure time for occupation or any other purposes.

CHAPTER 4

PROMINENT LIBRARIES IN THE WORLD

LIBRARY OF CONGRESS: The Library of Congress is the research library that officially serves the United States Congress and is the de facto National Library of the United States. It is the oldest federal cultural institution in the United States. Library of Congress is the second largest library in the world by a number of items with 164 million-plus. It is situated in Washington. It officially serves the Government of the United States.

NEW YORK PUBLIC LIBRARY: The New York Public Library is a public library system in New York. The New York Public Library is the second-largest public library in the United States and the third-largest in the world. It has 92 branches with more than 53 million books. New York Public Library has been an essential provider of free books, information, ideas and education. It was founded in 1895.

THE ROYAL LIBRARY: The Royal Library in Copenhagen is the National Library of Denmark and the University Library of the University of Copenhagen. It is among the largest libraries in the world and the largest in the Nordic countries. In 2017, it merged with the State and University Library to form a combined national library. It is the national library of Denmark. It was established in 1648. It has more than 35 million books. The Black Diamond in Copenhagen was finished in 1999 and is now an extension to the Royal Library.

THE BRITISH LIBRARY: The British Library is the National Library of the United Kingdom. It is the largest National Library in the world by a number of items catalogued. It is estimated to contain 150-200 million-plus items from all countries. It represents every age of written civilization. It is situated in London, UK. It offers a range of exhibitions. Some of them are free. The treasure gallery tells the remarkable study of over two thousand years of human experience. It also runs lively events and programmes.

BODLEIAN LIBRARY OF THE UNIVERSITY OF OXFORD: It is the main research library of the University of Oxford. It is one of the oldest libraries in Europe. It has over 12 million items. It is the second-largest library in Britain after the British Library.

STATE LIBRARY VICTORIA: It is in Australia. It is the Central Library of the State of Victoria located in Melbourne, Australia. It was established in 1854 as the Melbourne Public Library. It is Australia's oldest Public Library and one of the first free libraries in the world. Melbourne is a landmark and cultural icon. The State Library is a magnificent 19th-century building with some of the city's most beautiful heritage interiors. The State Library's collections include over two million books, hundreds of thousands of pictures, newspapers, maps and manuscripts; and masses of audios, videos, and digital material- all reflecting the culture of Victoria over the past 150 years.

Objectives of Public Library: Main objectives of Public Library are to provide resources to support and develop the knowledge and skill in the country. To contribute to the development of positive attributes to each student is the main objective. In addition, the prime objective of the library material is to provide materials that will stimulate students' acquisition of factual knowledge, development of literary appreciation, aesthetic values and ethical standards. The primary function of our library is to implement, enrich and support the educational programmes. It provides a wide range of material at various levels of sophistication with a diversity of appeal and different points of view.

The School Library provides comprehensive services related to the use of all types of material and equipment to support the instructional programme. Opportunities are provided for the students and teachers to read, listen and view; to prepare material and to work individually in small groups or in class groups. It provides guidance in the science of technology. It provides guidance in reading and listening; in reviewing media production. It maintains a carefully selected collection of instructional and recreational material- both print and non-print on all subjects appropriate to the interests of students.

It organizes materials, equipment, facilities and staff for prompt service related to the use of instructional material and equipment.

CHAPTER 5

ROLE OF LIBRARY

It is universally accepted in the modern socialistic era that all the people should have equal chances for their development in every walk of life. The bases of society are civilization, culture and collective feeling. Various defects or vices like laziness, ignorance and illiteracy are obstacles in the way of society's progress. The civilization, culture and collective feeling cannot be maintained and promoted until these are eradicated. As a result of these vices, society and nation remain unstable for the sake of progress and development of society. It is essential to remove these hindrances.

Every member of society must be literate and educated. Most of the people fail to be literate and educated due to ignorance and poverty. As such, it is the responsibility of the educated and intellectual classes of the society to make the illiterate people literate. This is the reason why all the new education methods are becoming library-oriented. In other words, education at any level is completely supplemented by the use of the library. People may be literate and educated through the medium of the library. They may be able to make their knowledge up-to-date through self-study.

Aim of Education: The main aim of education is to develop the whole personality of the people. It makes them capable of earning their livelihood, maintaining their existence in society and using their rights properly. Main objectives of education can be described as under:

1. Education relieves the members of the society of ignorance and superstition.
2. It develops the internal tendencies of the people. Education enhances their knowledge.
3. It develops a personality. It establishes peace and fraternity.It develops brotherhood feelings among people.

4. Education makes political, economic and scientific progress.

In this way, it is evident that education enables our society and nation to make progress in every field, including economic and scientific ones.

Liabilities: The libraries are entrusted with certain liabilities in the present society. Library executes the following functions:

i.   To keep the people aware of their rights and duties. The library keeps him acquainted with the latest information and matters.

ii. Library attracts the people during their leisure time and inspires them to study literature containing latest information, recreation and eternal knowledge.

iii. The modern library keeps the political ideology based on democracy in motion.

To perform the above functions in a well-organized way, it is essential to preserve the ancient and modern literature for the people of the present times and the coming generations. The literature is the carrier of information and knowledge. The idea of preserving study material has contributed to the growth of the library. One of the main functions of the library for the welfare of the society is to collect,arrange and preserve the study material. On this basis, the library collects, organizes and decentralizes the knowledge which is available but scattered.

Library strengthens the foundation of the nation and renders significant contribution in presenting it as a well-organized nation.

Purpose of Library: Libraries are repositories for the knowledge of humanity. They are our past, our present and our future. They are much more than storehouses for books. They include many other forms of data. The information available in libraries must be accessible to all people, regardless of education, age or economic status. Retrieval of particular types of information requires specialized knowledge and database searches that are beyond the capabilities of many users, and particularly of undergraduates starting their university careers. Librarians need to share that knowledge with users instructing them on how to use electronic, resources and the internet so that they can do research on their own while pointing out the limits and problems associated with electronic research. The library is also considered to be a part of the service sector. We are living in a world of change and uncertainty. Professionals who work for libraries have to learn the techniques of leadership methods. Main purposes of modern libraries are as under:

a. To make efforts for the expansion of literacy and education.
b. To put emphasis on self-study for the development of personality.
c. To teach the best utilization of leisure time.
d. To keep the knowledge of the people time up-to-date.
e. To collect and preserve useful literature.
f. To keep up the feelings of universal brotherhood.
g. To make efforts for social uplift and welfare.
h. To give protection and encouragement to research work by providing with the available data, facts and allied information.

Importance of Modern Libraries: The importance of modern libraries is enumerated below:

1. All-around Development of Personality- Library provides every person with an opportunity to make all-round development of his personality. By studying the study material collected and preserved in a library, a person can become adept in his work and prove himself helpful in the progress of the country besides his individual progress.
2. Research Work- As far as research work is concerned,thelibrary makes a collection of the whole

published study material at its earliest opportunity and makes the study material available to research scholars. The library helps a research student by providing him promptly with every new idea, information, data, etc.,concerned with his research work.

3. Collection and Preservation of Knowledge- The culture and civilization of a country can be evaluated on the basis of the libraries in that country. The ancient ideals and assumptions of the concerned country are evaluated. The ancient ideal remains alive in its library. The study material is collected and preserved in libraries so that the coming generations may be benefitted by it.

4. Cooperative in Self-study or Self-education- It is through the library that a person can get self-education lifelong.

5. Nation Building- In a library, knowledge and experience of political thinkers, social reformers and the learned are kept intact in the form of books and other study material. The person visiting the library may study the study material and get inspiration from it. It is also meant for the best use of leisure. One can enjoy healthy recreation.

Functions of Modern Libraries: Main functions of modern libraries are as under:

1. Collection, organization and preservation of study material.
2. To make the study material available on demand by the reader.
3. To arouse library consciousness in the people.

A library has to do the undermentioned work:

a. The work of survey and evaluation of new literature.
b. Reference service, collection of monthly lists and catalogues.
c. To cooperate with other libraries and exchange literature.

d. To enhance the present collection of books according to demand.

e. To cooperate in publication.

f. To perform extension services.

g. Writing and recording work for the preservation of research work.

h. To make efforts to develop reading tendency in the readers.

i. To do cooperative work. In fact, no library, however rich it may be, can satisfy all of its readers. So, it becomes indispensable to do cooperative work for the fulfilment of more and more readers.

CHAPTER 6

ACADEMIC LIBRARY: OBJECTIVES AND FUNCTIONS

Education is the main pillar of an educated society. The main objective of education is the all-round development ofpeople's personality.Education enables them to perform the functionssuch as to maintain their place in the society, to earn their livelihood, to learn the proper use of their rights, to keep immune of ignorance and superstitions, to develop their internal tendencies and to enhance their knowledge. The awareness of a society, its civilization and educative standard become evident from the "Education Policy" of that nation.

An educational institution is incomplete in the absence of a well-equipped library. The standard of a Nation's institutions providing higher education is determined on the basis ofthe books,magazines and research material available in the libraries.Main objectives of practical education are to keep students well-informed of the subjects under study, to make the intellectual powers aware of the latest development andto make them self-reliance in the field of education, etc. The educational institutions fulfilthe above objectives with the cooperation received from libraries.

Academic libraries are integral parts of the educational institutions. They give cooperation in the performance of educational institutions. The academic libraries are of three types:

a. School Libraries,
b. College Libraries, and
c. University Libraries.

Among the Academic libraries, School Library has the most significant position. School Library creates interest in a student's primary educational life towards study. If once this interest is created, it never dies. Instead, it develops more and more. According to M. P.

Douglas, a School Library is a scientific agency, a teaching agency, a study material collection centre, and an institution working as a study centre.

According to Douglas, a School Library performs the following functions:

1. A School Library plays a clear and active role in the teaching work.
2. It works as a study-material centre and provides the teachers and students with the desired books, magazines and allied material.
3. It acts as a study centre. It provides a proper place for the study of books and the solution of related problems. School Library is run by the school authority.
4. School Library tends help in the fulfilment of the objects of the school. It makes available textbooks, help books and allied necessary study material.

SIGNIFICANCE OF SCHOOL LIBRARY: A School Library can be called the heart of a school. In a library, the students enter with various kinds of experiences, problems and questions. The importance of a School Library may be explained as under:

1. Achievement of New Values:Inthe library, the students give solid forms to their intellectual tastes, and the capacities inherent in their aptitudes. On this basis, they get new social and educative values
2. To Give Reality: The libraries give solid reality to the efforts of the students made to give a solid basis to their intellectual tastes.
3. Laboratory: A School Library is the educational laboratory of the school. Here, both the teachers and the students get practical and current knowledge.

4. Education: For the fulfilment of educative purpose, a School Library is an important organ of the school.
5. Educational Communication: A library installs educational life in the schools
6. Nutrition: The library provides nutrition to the immature minds of students.
7. Means of Education: A School Library is accepted as a powerful means of education.
8. Wide Contacts: A school library brings the students into close contact with the learned, thinkers and scholars of local, national and international levels. The students come to learn new ideas and knowledge.
9. Self-study: The students fulfil their educational aptitude and are inspired for self-study.
10. Development of Talents: The present-day world is full of cut-throat competition. A student cannot get a proper place on the basis of only general knowledge. It is essential for him to develop his talents.
11. Medium for Progress: A School Library works as a powerful means for qualitative progress and development.
12. Measurementof Knowledge: A School Library provides measurement for the educational standard of that school.

OBJECTIVES OF SCHOOL LIBRARY: According to L.F. Forgo,there are undermentioned objectives of a school library:

Guidance to Students in the Selection of Study Material: A school aims at making the students able to choose good and proper study material and its constructive or positive use. But it is possible only when there is mutual cooperation between the teachers and the librarian. The students are in need of various kinds of study material. They need proper guidance in the selection of such study material. In this connection, the librarian has a major role to play. He may provide the students with the best guidance in selecting the study material. In this connection, an important duty of a librarian is to give the maximum guidance to the students in the formation of study planning. His proper guidance makes a student self-reliant in the selection of the study material.

Proper Arrangement of the Material: School Library makes the collection of the best and useful study material as well as arranges in a proper way. The librarian classifies the study material and thereafter prepares catalogues. This system enables students to utilize that study material easily.

Arrangement for Books and other Study Material: According to the necessity of the syllabus, aSchool Library makes the collection of the study material. It tries to make out the aptitude of the students and collect the useful study material.

To Inculcate the Study Aptitude: A School Library inculcates study aptitude in the students. Besides, it gives maximum help in the development of their interest in the study. Like other habits, the habit of book-reading may be inculcated from childhood itself. In present times, there is a literature explosion. A student can gain knowledge from the study material available in the library.

To Encourage for Self-Study and Life-Long Education: A library arouses skill in the students to use books. With it, the students have a life long aptitude for studying books and their wide use. In this connection, a School Library makes students self-reliant and self-dependent. Besides, it creates in them desire to feel the pleasure gained from self-study.

Cooperation with Educational and Administrative Staff: A School Library gives maximum possible cooperation to the staff connected with imparting education. In this way, it creates a sense of responsibility in them. A School Library gives cooperation to the students in books selection.

Proper Utilization of Time: A School Library creates the feeling of proper utilization of time in the students. It procures study material according to the aptitude of the students. It creates in them the habit of proper use of time.

Functions of School Library: A School Library establishes coordination among the variouseducational functions of school and makes efforts to achieve the school's objectives. Besides it, by doing the works for the achievement of educational objectives, it tries to justify its important place in the school.

Enhancement in Information:A School Library provides the students with various kinds of information through books. It provides the students with information of various kinds and in variouswalks of life.

To Make Inspiring Books Available: When students study some books available in the School Library, they are bound to take some inspiration from them.Thereafter, they try to mould themselves accordingly.

To Help in Self-Study: A School Library arouses in the student's inclination towards self-study. An ideal student studies something in the class. Thereafter, he goes to the library and widens his knowledge on that topic with the help of other books. A School Library creates a healthy habit of self-study in the students.

Inspiration to Participate in Extra-Curricular Activities: A School Library inspires the students to participate in various extra-curricular activities arranged in school, e.g. plays, debates and other competitions. It is rich with the autobiographies and biographies of great persons besides other inspiring study material.

Utilization of Library: The School Library gives training to the students astohow to utilize the study material collected and preserved in the library. Some examples are as to get the study material by using catalogues and utilizing various reference books. With the help of this training acquired in the School Library, the students become capable of using public libraries and professional or occupational libraries easily.

Proper Utilization of Books: The library stafftrains the readers on how to utilize the books properly. Some books are complicated in their utilization. The library staff gives ample information to the students astohow to go through those books. In this way, gradually,the students become capable of utilizing books properly and easily. Various rules are framed to utilize the books in libraries. Thus, the students learn the utilization of books under those rules.

Social Point of View: Besides the development of morality, a library inculcates such habits in the students as are necessary from a social point of view. Some of these views are as under:

   i.   The books should not be soiled.
   ii.   Their pages should not be torn and removed.
   iii.   The books should not be stolen from the library.
   iv.   The books borrowed from the library should be returned in time so that other readers may not suffer.

Silent Reading: The students study books together in a library. It inculcates in them the habit of studying together peacefully. This habit contributes to the development of their mind.

Utilization of Time: Whenever a student has spare time, he may go to the library and study the recreational or inspiring books as he wishes. If the library has a rich collection of the study material which interests the students most, they will certainly go to the library to utilize their spare time and study that material. It will inculcate the habit of reading in them. It will help themin determining the course of their life in the future.

Helpful in Intellectual Development of the Teacher: Besides contributing to the mental development of the students, the School Library tries a lot to the intellectual development of teachers. When teachers visit the library, they are attracted by various books on different subjects. They go through the books on their subjects as well as another subject. Thus, they widen and deepen their knowledge. As a result, they gain mastery over the subject. By improving their expression, they are in a position to present their topic in the classroom more clearly and successfully.

To conclude, it can be said that a School Library aims at helping in the evaluation, coordination and development of the personal capacities of each and every student.

CHAPTER 7

COLLEGE AND UNIVERSITY LIBRARY

COLLEGE LIBRARY: A college is called the entrance to higher education. It is from here that the depth study of a subject begins. The main function of the College Library is to complete the educational task. It is the pivot of all the educational activities of the college.

FUNCTIONS: According to Loyal, main functions of a College Library are as under:

1. To assist in the educational activities through reference service.
2. To inspire the students to study useful books in greater number.
3. To make available the library services in departmental members for the purpose of raising the educational standard.
4. To contribute to the development of educational activities.

OBJECTIVES: Main objectives of the College Library are as under:

1. Development: To make the intelligence of the students penetrating, to widen their attitude and develop their memory.
2. Cooperation: To cooperate with the teachers in studying and teaching.
3. Emphasis on self-study: To put emphasis on self-study in the field of education to make the readers self-reliant and self-made.
4. To enhance the general knowledge and education.
5. Multi-books oriented: To make the reader's book-oriented in greater number and on various subjects.

6. Wide and comparative: To give a wide and comparative form to education through individual services and guidance.

UNIVERSITY LIBRARY: A university can be called the main seat of higher education and research work. In a university, special mastery is obtained on the desired topic. This centre is a way of knowledge and science. Besides, here is knowledge decentralized. The preservation and development of knowledge are based on university education.

INGREDIENTS: For the implementation of the objectives of education, the following four ingredients are essential:

i. Able students
ii. Teachers
iii. Laboratory, and
iv. Library.

University Education Commission has expressed its views about library like this:"Teaching is a cooperative task. A library is the heart of all the functions of the library. Such a form of a library is evident directly from the research point of view and indirectly from the point of view of other works."

Wilson Louts and Tower opine that the fulfilment of the objectives of universities is based on the libraries connected with them. A University Library collects and arranges books manuscripts, magazines and allied material and helps in the expansion programme of the university.

Kothari Commission has laid more emphasis on the necessity of libraries in colleges and universities. In its opinion, "A university or a college should not be permitted to start the study of a new subject until the library staff is satisfied with the number of necessary books and magazines on the subject."

ROLE OF UNIVERSITY LIBRARY: During the present day, the responsibility of the library has increased many times. In nearly every university, there is a well-equipped library. In university, the students make study and gain mastery over their desired subjects and topics. A library is a way to knowledge. It is the main centre for the decentralization of knowledge.The preservation or conservation of knowledge and its development is based on university education. In a university, a library acts as the heart. Without a well-furnished library, the university looks inactive. According to Wilson and Tower, the modern university has several types of functions as under:

    i.   Extension of Education and Knowledge
   ii.   Explanation
  iii.   Research
   iv.   Publication
    v.   Teaching
   vi.   Conservation of Knowledge, and
  vii.   Ideas.

University needs to take the help of the library to perform the above important functions. University is based on the library. The reason is that only through a rich and up-to-date library, higher education and research work is possible. It is only with the help of a library that ancient and modern knowledge and ideas are to be preserved. In the absence of cooperation by the library, teaching, research and publication work cannot be possible at all.

FUNCTIONS OF UNIVERSITY LIBRARY: According to the Kothari Education Commission, the main functions of University Library are enumerated below:

University Library works as a media contact between departmental libraries and study centre. It provides aid to Research Scholars in their research work. It provides requisite means and facilities for research work in the topics of regional value. Library obtains cooperation from the various Heads of Departments and frames coordination programmes for the development of the library. It brings the books, students and the learned into close contact. It stirs intellectual curiosity. It arouses the tendency for research.

Information: Library renders necessary information to the professors regarding further development in their respective subjects. The Parry Committee enumerated the following functions of the University Library:

a. To maintain information about useful publications.
b. To obtain necessary literature from the publications.
c. To obtain individual collections of the learned, and to conserve these collections. The purpose is to keep safe the ancient achievements and values for the coming generations.
d. To make available the library services to the learned, scholars and scientists outside the university.
e. University Library arranges necessary literature for the students and the scholars to fulfil undermentioned objectives:

i. Reading in the classroom.
ii. Students'participation in seminars.
iii. For self-study.

a. University Library establishes new departments. It provides scholars and professors with the necessary research material for pursuing further studies.
b. University Library gives training to the undergraduates who are desirous of making critical self-study.
c. University Library provides with necessary study catalogue for training on a priority basis or on a normal basis

CHAPTER 8

NATIONAL LIBRARY

National Library is the supreme library of the Nation. According to the UNESCO, the National Library is the library which is responsible for the receipt and preservation of all the books, magazines and other printed study material published in the country. It works under the law as a collection library. Dr Ranganathan opines that National Library is the library which bears the liability of collecting and preserving the published works and manuscripts of the country for the use by the public at large. The National Library is the supreme centre of the public library system.It is the guardian of all libraries. It has the coordination between all libraries. It also works as a copyright library. It is a source of availability of rare literature. It is the decentralization of knowledge on a national level. It is the national compiler of books catalogue.

FUNCTIONS OF NATIONAL LIBRARY: It works as Inter-Library Exchange. It does the work of lending books through Regional Central Libraries on the national level and through National Central Libraries at international level. It renders special library services for VIP classes. It collects important publications. It is the recipient of all the published literature in the country free of any charges. It has a compilation of books catalogue. It prepares a catalogue of two types- National Catalogue and International Bibliography. It works as cooperative classification and codification at the national level with cooperation of the publications at large.

The National Library also renders reference and information services. It is the liability of the National Library to make available these books. The National Library supplies the libraries, administrative bodies and scholars with needed information.

It carries various coordination works such as publishing magazines, highlighting the research work and various experiments. It sends experts to libraries in other parts of the country. It makes arrangement for a professional conference and seminar.

The National Library in India is situated in Calcutta. Before independence, its name was Imperial Library. In 1948, the Government of India named it National Library. According to the Books Delivery Act, 1954 and 1956, this library is a Copyright Library. One copy each of every published book all over India is recovered by this library free of charge. Main magazines published in the country and abroad are available here. There is a collection of manuscripts and rare literature. Government publications in millions are available here.

The National Library has a well-equipped reading hall with the seating capacity of hundreds of readers at a time. Reference service is provided here. There is inter-libraries exchange on a national and international level. The National Library receives foreign publications through numerous agencies situated in several counties.Catalogue of Subject Headings, Catalogue of Indian Books and Catalogue of Indian Writers, are its main publications. However, some critics say that:

a. It is a National Library in the name only.
b. It does not compile regularly the International Catalogue.
c. It does not exchange the books on an international level.
d. The National Catalogue is not up-to-date.
e. All the publishers do not send copies of the published books to it free of cost.

Hence, it is essential to seek the attention of the Government towards it and efforts should be made so that the National Library can work effectively

CHAPTER 9

PUBLIC LIBRARY: IMPORTANCE AND FUNCTIONS

A Public Library is the library which is run by the people in the interest of the people. A Public Library makes available study material to every class community, sex, caste and age without any discrimination. B. S. Russel has defined Public Library as "Public body run by the public for the welfare of the public."According to C. G.Vishwanathan, "A Public Library is one which is managed by the local authority and fed completely or partially with its own resources. It is administered by some Authority or Committee. Its aim is to provide all the citizens of its area with its services, free of charge having no consideration to caste, colour or any other distinction."

PURPOSE: Main purposes of a Public Library are as under:

1. Collection, preservation and distribution of study material for the progress of people at large.
2. Service of every member of the society with the collected study material.

In this way, it can be said that the Public Library is the library of the people. Main objectives of a Public Library are as under:

i. To achieve the objectives of cent per cent literacy in the country.
ii. Preservation of all means of culture and civilization.
iii. To encourage enlightened citizenship and prosperous personal life.
iv. To keep the people acquainted with the utility of books.
v. To create curiosity in people to increase their demand for books.
vi. To keep society acquainted with democratic ideologies.

Functions and Importance of Public Libraries:

1. Literacy: Library is useful not only for literate people but also for illiterate ones. It helps the illiterates in becoming literate. Hence,the books are read overto illiterates. Besides various means like movies, radio and television are used to make the people literate.

2. Aid to Basic Education: The basic education is the minimum and general education which aims at helping those children, youths and elderly people who are unable to get even primary education. The basic education enables them to understand their rights and duties as citizens. Thus, they become capable of playing their role in a more impressive away in the economic and social progress of their community.

3. Collection and Preservation of Knowledge: One can evaluate the culture and civilization of a country on the basis of that country's libraries. The library has the living testimony or pictures of the ancient ideas and assumptions of that country. A library collects and preserves the ancient and rare books which are the cultural and literary treasure of the past. It aims at benefitting the coming generations and the research work of the contemporary society.

4. Public Library: According to the UNESCO, Public Library is a conscious power for mass education. Today, it is accepted beyond any discussion or doubt that a library is the main and active means for public education and public consciousness. Today, the library not only performs the exchange of books but also creates a desire in the people to attain more and more knowledge. The libraries are the storehouses of wisdom.

5. Life-Long Self-Education: No person can get life long education from any college or university. However, he can add to his knowledge by becoming a member of a Public Library.

6. Research Work: Every research scholar enjoys the liberty to get the maximum advantage of the study material collected and preserved in public libraries. In a Public Library, every kind of published study material is collected promptly. When demanded, this material is made available to the research scholar. A Public Library accords its fullest cooperation to a research scholar by making available any latest material concerning his research work.

7. National and International Cooperation: Public libraries are helpful in increasing mutual co-operation and goodwill, national unity and cooperation. In fact, they are living power for mass education.It is the library that can remove the darkness of illiteracy and light the illuminating lamp of life-long education. The library service can arouse the feeling of political, national and educative consciousness by making the mass educated. Dr S.Ranganathan has said, "The functions of a library are inclusive of educative, constructive, political, economic, technical, cultural and archaeological."

8. Best Utilization of Leisure: A library gives the opportunity to the people to make the best use of their leisure.It provides them with healthy recreation. All the people of any age, e.g. children, young ones and elderly ones may visit the library and make the best use of their leisure by getting and going through literature according to their choice. Library arranges from time to time various kinds of educative movies, plays and other kinds of gatherings. Thus, it provides visitors with healthy recreation.

9. Nation Building: The knowledge and experiences, as well as views of the nation's learned scholars, political thinkers and social reformers, are preserved in the books and other study material maintained in the library. People may study this material, get knowledge and inspiration from it and make

their moral and intellectual development. The library contributes help to the moral and intellectual development of a nation.

10. The success of Democracy: The position and number of libraries in anycountry can tell about the future of democracy in that country. The expansion of democratic thoughts in the masses is the basis of the democratic success of that country. The library is the only place where these ideas and thoughts may flourish. The libraries have a collection of study material and by giving the knowledge of good and bad; they keep the masses conscious and awaken. They are helpful in enabling people to perform their duties and be conscious of their rights.

11. All-Round Development of Personality: Every reader who visits a library gets an opportunity for all-round development of his personality. Anybody may go through the study material collected and maintained in a library. By doing so, he may become adept in his profession, and thus,hecan not only make his own progress but also contribute to the progress of the nation. Public libraries are a significant means of a country's prosperity. They are essential for the progress of civilization and education of society. Such libraries prove helpful to man in his life-struggle.

CHAPTER 10

LIBRARY PROFESSION

LouisAAllen opines that the library profession is a special kind of act which is performed with the use of systematic knowledge and general diction. It needs a moral code propounded by specified measurements and recognized institutions. A library profession is an industry. It requires special knowledge and long term and serious preparations. It needs training for understanding the scientific, historical and scholarly principles of its functions and techniques. It is based on organized and solid high-class achievements and management. It engages its members in continuous study and public service-oriented special functions.

To conclude, it can be said that a library profession is an act where knowledge and experience offer services to people in society. The person engaged with the profession has to obtain permission from some controlling institution. He has to abide by the general moral code prescribed by the institution.

In-library profession, a specified course is to be studied. A person connected with the profession has special knowledge of his work.Training and experience in the profession is a definite and prescribed one. Every profession has its code of conduct. Special emphasis is laid on the feeling to serve in the profession. The library profession is not intended for one's own self but for other persons.

The basis of library science is psychological. The library profession is utilized for all people in society. The library profession is a proper means for earninga livelihood. Library organizations are established for the development of libraries.

It can be said that a profession is that group of efficient and organized persons which remains in the service of the people of a particular area. The group of efficient persons who are organized and engrossed in library services is called the library profession. Its members are efficient in library science. Simultaneously, they have knowledge of more than one subject. Thus, a librarian arranges the study material available in the library scientifically.

Like other prestigious professions, library science is an honourable means of earning money and livelihood. No industry can make any progress without the cooperation of the library. The people connected with this profession should have ample knowledge and certain qualities. In their absence, library science will lose its progress. Their qualities are as under:

    i.   Acquaintance with the sources of knowledge.
   ii.   Professional efficiency and politeness.
  iii.   Attention and sincerity.
  iv.   Aptitude for studies.
   v.   Knowledge of the value of time.

However, it should be born in mind that the library profession does not fetch much money. It can only be a source of earning a livelihood. Yet, by getting knowledge through it continuously, a person feels an expressible joy.

CHAPTER 11

FIVE LAWS OF LIBRARY SCIENCE

ShiyaliRamamritaRanganathanis considered as the "Father of Library Science." He believed that there are certain essential principles underlying the management of the library according to the present dayneed and conception. He expounded these principles in a methodical form and reduced them to five cardinal principles. He has developed all these rules of library organization and management as the necessary implications and the inevitable corollary of his five laws.

According to Dr S. R. Ranganathan, there are five laws of library science. The statements embodying these laws were formulated in1928, and a detailed account of these laws and their implications were published in the form of a book in 1931 by the Bombay Asia Publishing House. Basically, these laws are:

1. Books are there for use.
2. Every reader must have his book.
3. Every book has its reader.
4. Save the time of the reader.
5. The library is a rising organism.

FIRST LAW: The first law explains an elementary principle. All the other laws of library science are based on it. It is seen that a library becomes great not because of its collection or building but because of the user. The motto of a librarian must be to acquire books related information and serve documents for use. A modern librarian who has belief in first law will feel satisfied only if the user keeps the shelves constantly empty. According to Dr Ranganathan, the implications of first law are:

Location of the Library: The important partof the library is its location. Locationof the library should be approachable and accessible to the community. Public Library should be placed where more citizens can frequently visit regularly on some business or another day. At the same time, the location should beasfree from noise and other disturbances as possible so that serious study can be made. It is found that the University Library should be centrally located. A special library should be near the factory entrance or factory canteen. A library of school or college does not depend on location as distances are small from various sections. However, it would be preferable to have it centrally located.

Library Building and Furniture: The structure of the library should be well planned. Its interior should be inviting and attractive. The building should be functional and at the same time, visual. The position of the library should be functional that should provide enough space for various purposes to meet the requirements. The furniture should be provided so as to give comfort to the readers and to make use of the resources such as the books should not be kepthigh, and books on the top shelves should be easily reachable.

Library Working Hours: The working hours of the library should be decided to keep in view the need of the readers. The first law results in the opening library for long hours and on all days of the year without any holidays. Its hours should be convenient for users. It is recommended that each user of the library should be provided with a key so that the user can use the library at any time.

Library Staff: For the best use of the library, it is believed that it should run with qualified and efficient staff. Over there in the library, every staff member should perform the role of a friend, philosopher and guide to all who comes to use it. The staff should believe in and follow the philosophy of service to the user. They should be approachable, courteous, helpful and willing to appreciate the point of views of others. A mission by the zeal to serve the user, amicable manners and professional capability are the essential truths of the library staff for carrying out the mandate of the first law.

Book Selection: The books should be selected and acquired, keeping in view the present and potential requirement of the user. There shouldbe periodical weeding out of books.

Shelf Arrangement: The bookshelf design should be classified, catalogued and arranged according to the helpful sequence.

Reference Service: The personal service will lead to great use of library document. The forces of the first law can be looked at from the following:

It was observed that in ancient period, books were rare, i.e. multiple copies were not available due to the non-availability of printing machine. It is seen that copying of the Mahabharata was very tough, requiring long hours to copy a document. So, in the past, there was a great deal of negligence towards the first law. In recent times, because of the availability of printing technology, photocopying orscanning is possible to overcome all such barriers. It was observed that the forces of the first law could be traced out by:

a. Making the library open access and not cloud access;
b. Giving free access to the book world;
c. Branching libraries in larger cities in order to easily reachable within a few minutes walk from each house;
d. Delivering books free to the houses of those that would offer to get introduced in their neighbourhood;
e. Distribution books in a motor van from street to street for the residents.

It was believed that these above forces of first law would be possible only if the library has enough funds and can itself obtainafree copy of books from different sources. In this commercial world, everybody pays according to higher need or requirement, or there is a doubt that an exception will happen for library and information science.

SECOND LAW: The second law states that every reader must have his book and believed that books are for all. In this law, every reader of the library should have books of his requirement. It advocates for a mandatory provision of library services to each reader according to his need. It advocates the universal and democratization of library services, i.e. documents are not merely for scholars but for all including the poor, sick, blind, prisoner, neo-literates and the old. The document should be easy to get irrespective of the occupational income lines; irrespective of an adult and a child. After this, Ranganathan examines the implications of the second law as:

a. The obligation of the State:

Library Legislation: It is found that in order to achieve the second law, it is desirable that economy factor should be considered and should not act as a barrier. This was only possible by way of library legislation which provides finance of public libraries at various levels to achieve free library services for all.

Maintenance of Library System: It was believed that with respect to students, teachers and researchers, the public library plays a marginal role in fulfilling the second law as the state has the responsibility of establishing other types of libraries such as school library, a college library,theuniversity library and special library.

Coordination and Resource Sharing:A given library would not have the finance to purchase documents on occasional demand. Hence, the second law suggests the formulation of a national library network to share resources, especially for the purpose of inter-library loan.

b. The obligation of the Library Authority:

Choice of the Book: AS per second law, it was believed that all the books that can be useful should be selected and all useful books should be discarded. The selection of books should be based on individual needs. It is the duty of the library authority to ensure that proper selection and acquisition policy should be there in order tobuild up a balanced collection in the library for each category of users, i.e. the blind, neo-literates, scholars, children, young, adult, man, woman, etc.

Buying a document that has no potential demand is a violation of the second law.

Choice of the Staff: According to the second law, the library authority should select an adequate and competent team of library staff that should take utmost care in recruiting the library personnel, their subsequent promotion, recognition and status.

c. The obligation of the Library Staff:

Open Access: It was found that the library staffshould feel the obligation to introduce open access to help the readers in gaining access to all books of their interest. The open-access makes it possible for a reader to approach books directly and handle them personally without any barrier. Through open access, a user can browse amongst the world of books and thus will have better chances of choosing the right books.

Cataloguing: It is seen that manytimes, the information contained in a chapter of a book may be of interest to a reader, but the users often tend to miss such content. To avoid this,thelibrary should introduce subject analytical or cross-reference entries.

Arrangement: In libraries, the shelf should be arranged according to the subject of the document and not on the size and other aspects.

Maintenance: Maintenance is important in the library. In case of open-access libraries, there is every possibility of some document being misplaced intentionally or unintentionally by the patron of the library. To fulfil the second law, misplaced books must be restored to their proper place. Books in need of binding or repair should be taken out from the shelves from time to time.

Reference Service: Reference service is an effective means of ensuring that the reader gains access to all the documents of potential interest to him that are held by the library. So, the library staff should have proper training in reference work and be able to provide effective reference service to the user in getting the right book.

d. The obligation of the Reader:

Library Rules to be Followed: Rules are an important aspect in every library. A reader must realize that library rules are framed to get the maximum out of the library resources and to prevent the exploitation of library resources. The rules are aimed at increasing the use of the library rather than curbing its use. Thus, the user should regard the enforcement of the rules as an aid rather than a hindrance in the use of the library.

Maintenance of the System:A library should have a good maintenance system. A user should know how to keep his books. He should not misplace the book or damage it. A user should not injure or take out cards from the library catalogue, tear pages or steal.

Undue Privileges Unwanted: Library is there for the use of an individual and no one should have unwanted privileges at the cost of others. The current issues, the reference books, etc. which are in much demand should not go through the process of any special privileges.

Return of Books in Time: Issuing date and delivery date play an important role in the library. The books issued must be returned on or before the due date so that other users do not have to suffer. If a document or book is lying unused at home, it is the obligation of the user to return it as soon as possible.

THIRD LAW: The third law states that every book in a library must find its reader. This law emphasizes the approach to the document. As per this law, all books in a library must have their distinct readers. Not a single item should be lost in the darkness of the stock. To give more effect to this law, the following measures should be adopted:

Introducing Open Access: In the case of the open access system, books are arranged in shelves in the classified order, and the readers have the liberty to access them. In the course of reader's browsing through the shelves, they may come across books of interest to them, the existence of which they may not be aware of. So, the chances of readers noticing the books and reading them are enhanced by the open access system only.

Provision of Popular Department: There should be a provision of popular departments such as newspaper reading room, periodical section, etc. which could offer baits to the readers and the benefit of such provision is to increase the chances for every book to get its reader. Recent editions, rare books, special collection, festival collection, etc. displayed at prominent places attract the reader's attention.

Book Selection: While selecting a book, attention should be paid so that the chances of books remaining unused are reduced.

Cataloguing: There should be a proper listing of items. Subject cataloguing, series entries, cross-reference entries, etc. may often disclose to the reader the books which might not have otherwise been noticed.

Shelf Arrangement: In case of proper shelf arrangement, the books can be arranged subject wise and title wise so that it gives readers better chances of finding books. In this case, the subsequent attention should be given by the library staff to maintain the arrangements by way of restoring the misplaced books to their correct place and so on.

Reference Service: Every reader should be provided with a reference staff that can guide fortaking proper caring of the books. Every librarymusthave provision for personal assistance to each reader when they feel they need it. The reference staff acts as a canvassing agent for the book.

Publicity and Library Extension Services: It is believed that within the premises of the library, the staff should provide shelf guide and bay guide thatguides the reader to appropriate places in the library. Externally, the reference staff should make the use of mass media such as press, radio, television, lecture, demonstrations, tours, exhibitions, library weeks, brochure, leaflets, etc. for publicizing the library.

FOURTH LAW: The fourth law explains the importance of the user. The law states that a user is supposed to be a busy person. So, his time should be saved. A reader coming to the library should get an exact and fast service. They should not be made to wait longer than necessary. Unnecessary delay may cause vexation and readers may be dissatisfied. Unhappy readers may cease to come to the library. We see the implications of the fourth law as under:

a. Location of Library: It was observed that the library must be centrally located so that it is conveniently accessible to the community being served.

b. Open Access: Open access plays an important role in the proper running of the library. There are many advantages of introducing open access. Once such advantage of open access system is the subjective time decline, which gives satisfaction to the readers.

c. ClassificationandCataloguing:Proper classification system should be employed, which would bring the documents together on a specific subject and also the related subject should be adopted.

d. Shelf Arrangement: The arrangement of the documents according to the degree of mutual relationship of subjects would lead to saving the time of the reader.

e. Charging System: The issuance, charging and discharging should be done as quickly as possible.

f. Information Technology: There should be a proper use of information technology in libraries in order to increase speed andtechnology. The fourth law signifies IT.

FIFTH LAW: The main mechanism of a library is documents, users and staff. A library always grows in terms of documents, the readers and the staff. The growth of a new library can be compared to the growth of a child as it grows in every aspect. In case of a service librarythat has attained a certain degree of stability; its growth can be compared to the growth of an adult. In this case, it grows in terms of replacing old documents by new ones and new users continuously replace the old ones. The implications of the fifth law are:

a. Library Building: As per the fifth law, the library building should be modular and should have the provision of future growth.

b. Choice of Classification and Cataloguing Code: The classification and cataloguing scheme chosen should have the provision to keep pace with the development in the universe of the subject.

c. Physical Forms of Catalogue: Itis found that the physical forms of catalogue chosen should have the provision of updating, sorting in a different order, editing, and so on.

d. Weeding Out of Document: For proper spacing, the documents that are obsolete and unused should be weeded out. This document should be stored where they are available for occasional use or as a central place with cooperation among libraries.

e. Modernization,Computerization: Libraries should be built with modern structures and should equip with the latest computational technique. Bigger libraries should be computerized so that it should support proper ordering and maintenance. In order to take care of the growing collection, the documents should be dignified or microfilmed; the new procurement should be made in the form of electronic journals, e-book, etc. To cope with the increased readership, the library should go for the video terminal and ultimately to the digital and virtual library.

Earlier the libraries grew with the collection. But nowadays the digital library, virtual library ore-library does not show the characteristics of the growth of a library by volume. The growth is in the use of sophisticated technologies.

Summing Up: It is seen that five laws of library science consist of five short statements, but they provide guidance and rationale for practice and teaching of library and information science. Based on these laws, we can derive postulates, cannons and principles applicable in different fields of library and information science. It was found that the first three laws emphasize the exploitation of the documents of the library by the maximum number of users,while the fourth law emphasizes on the role of a reference librarian and has a great potentiality to bring reforms in the running of libraries. It was observed that on the whole, all laws would serve as a source of inspiration and guidance in the years to come.

CHAPTER 12

POSITION AND FUNCTIONS OF LIBRARIAN

Alibrarian is a person who works professionally in a library, providing access to information and sometimes social or technical programming to users. In additions, librarians provide instruction and information literally.

Duties and Functions: Traditionally, a librarian is associated with collection of books demonstrated by the etymology of the word"Librarian." The role of a librarian is continually evolving to meet social and technological needs. A modern librarian may deal with provision and maintenance of information in many formats, including books, electronic resources, magazines, newspapers, audio and video recordings, maps, manuscripts, photographs and other graphical materials.

Librarian is considered as the authorized representative of the library. He is expected to keep good relation with all types of people who are engaged in the activities of the university.

There is a certain policy in every administration for the smooth functioning of the system. In-library administration, too, the policy is formed for various activities carried out in the library. The librarian has specialization in library science. He helps the members of the library committee and plays an important role in the formulation of policy. The librarian helps and suggests the library committee in preparation of the annual budget for the library. It is the library authority which approves the budget. The librarian gets the approval needed.

The highest official of an institution is its administrator. The administrator appoints the librarian and keeps direct contact with him. The librarian is directly responsible to the administrator. He brings the activities in the library to the knowledge of the administrator.

The administrator does the following functions through proper channel after obtaining the consent of the librarian:

I. Appointment of all employees of the library, their promotions, demotion, suspension or removal, if such a situation arises.

II. Keeping contact with the Academic Council, Executive Council, teachers, etc. The librarian is in direct contact with the members of the Academic Council, the Executive Council and teachers of the university. He plays a very important role when the Academic Council designs the syllabus.

III. He maintains close contact with the teachers of the university. This is done in order to keep the library useful for research, study and teaching.

In a nutshell, the librarian functions as a link officer between the Library Authority and the Library Committee. It becomes evident from the above that a librarian plays a vital role in the library administration.

CHAPTER 13

LIBRARY PROFESSIONALS ASSOCIATION

Meaning: An association is the group of those persons who are organized to fulfil some common objectives. In this way, the association is a group of persons who have faith in similar ideas and objectives.

In these days,theorganization is needed in every field. No work can be done well in the absence of organization. The main objective of the Library Association is to remove ignorance and illiteracy. An association has the following objectives:

a. To secure the rights of the members.
b. To give cooperation in the progress of profession and the nation.
c. To have control over the members with the help of the code of conduct.
d. To pay attention to professional development.

In this way, an association makes every possible effort to further its profession and inspire the members for dedication without any selfish motives.

The Library Association is essential for the progress of library movement. This is the obligation of the Government of India and the State Governments to encourage well-known and strong Library Associations. The Government should give financial aid to the Library Associations for the fulfilment of their objectives. The Advisory Committee for Library enumerated the undermentioned five functions of Library Association:

i. To upgrade the training of the librarian.
ii. To be helpful in the formation of a code of conduct towards

the community in the minds of the librarians.
iii. To create the feeling of fraternity in the librarians.
iv. To make a standard carrier of expansion.
v. To struggle for the improvement in the service condition of librarians. The Library Association works as a labour union.

Chief Functions: The Library Association performs the following functions:

a. To increase the library activities for the development of the libraries.
b. To arrange for the publication of periodicals for the advantages of the library profession and professional personnel.
c. To prepare a list of the persons who are trained in library science.
d. To perform some special professions, e.g. to prepare complete catalogues and bibliographies.

Library Professionals Association (LPA) is a registered society under the Society Registration Act constituted by the Government of India. The Association is for encouragement, development and support to the Library and Information Science (LIS) professionals in India through free communication, organizing seminars,conferences,meetings,trainingcourses, practical workshops, providing manpower support and other short term educational activities and orientation programmes with the help of new emerging information technologies. Training courses, seminars, workshops, practical orientation courses, lectures, etc. are being organized for a sufficient workforce of competent professionals by the Association from time to time. LPA has been organizing every year its annual conference on "Knowledge Organization in Academic Libraries" under the different theme of the conference since 2012 in various reputed organizations.

Conference Objectives: Main objectives of the conference are as under:

a. To discuss the rising contemporary issues related to Librarianship Development.
b. Increase recognition of support forexperimentation with innovative andtransformational ideas.
c. Help libraries and information centres make use of new and emerging technologies by promoting and supportingtechnological experimentation and innovation.
d. Increase leadershipdevelopment and training opportunities designed to support the ongoing transformation of libraries.

RANGANATHAN RAJYA PUSTAKALAYA SAMITI: Dr RanganathanRajyaPustakalaySamiti, Muzaffarpur is a registered society under Section 21 of Society Registration Act, 1860. This society was registered on 12 Jan 2016. The basic objectivesof the Society are:

a. To fulfil the social, educational, cultural, intellectual, ethical and artistic developmentof people living in the whole Bihar, and especially in Muzaffarpur district and spread the knowledge of library science.
b. To disseminate the promotion of education, literature and scientific knowledge and to make available books, articles, knowledgebooks and competition-related books to prepare for all types of competition examinations in school, college and to publish publication of manuscripts.
c. Organizing seminars and workshops for enhancing knowledge book and capacity building of common people.
d. Considering the environment of every district level library,

paving the way for its upgradation, consulting the curriculum studied, serving literature, collaborating in book publication and conducting book collection campaigns.

e. It will be our implication to encourage children, parents, teachers and governments to make successful cooperation from primary education to higher education, disseminating welfare education, promoting ethical education, and making school and technology education easy, inclusive and interesting.

CHAPTER 14

ETHICS OF AMERICAN LIBRARY ASSOCIATION

The American Library Association Committee on Professional Ethics produced a sample set of code of ethics. Most of the statements in the American Library Association's Code of Ethics encompass various ethical concerns that may arise from social media use.

Social media is defined by Merriam Webster Dictionary as "Forms of electronic communication through which users create online communication to share information, ideas, personal message, and other contents. Libraries participate in social media for many reasons but primarily to communicate information about library services and resources and to engage with their communities. Libraries also provide users with access to social media. And library workers often provide assistance to social media users.

While social media has created unprecedented opportunities for information sharing and for community building and engagement, it has also raised numerous ethical concerns. Such concerns include professional responsibility of staff- how the staff interacts with the public; how the staff interacts with the library privacy and data protection behaviour of professional library workers, and professional discourse with their colleagues, etc. Use of social media may affect the overall image of our profession and the public image of each institution.

American Library Association (ALA) promotes the creation, maintenance, and enhancement of a learning society. It ensures that public, academic and special libraries in every community may cooperate in providing lifelong learning services to all.

American Library Association treats co-workers and other colleagues with respect, fairness and good faith. It advocates for such condition of employment that may safeguard the rights and welfare of all employees of our institutions. Library workers should be cognizant of who may see or share their goals. Individuals should take responsibility for all online behaviours.

Library workers have an ethical responsibility to represent themselves and their colleagues, institutions and associations in both their professional and personal lives with respect, courtesy, sensitivity and fairness. Losing sight of their responsibility can lead to an ethical violation in the form of social media insensitive to colleagues, which may damage the reputation of all those involved. It protects each library user's right to privacy and confidentiality with respect to information sought or received or resources consulted, borrowed, acquired or transmitted.

As with anything regarding user information, libraries should keep the ALA Code of Ethics in mind as well as the State and Federal Law regarding patron privacy and the collection and use of personally identifiable information. It is the best to stay away from gathering information such as names, address, email address, social media handles and user names, social security number, date of birth, bank account information, or credit card information unless it is necessary for the provision of library services. The library has a special obligation to protect the privacy of itsusers. As the library is a trustedsource of information in our communities, the information shared through the library's social media outlets may carry more weight. For that reason, it is important to be thoughtful about what contents are shared.

American Library Association does not advance private interests at the expense of library users, colleagues or its employing institutions. It distinguishes between its personal convictions and professional duties and does not allow its personal belief to interfere with fair representation of the aims of its institutions or the provisions of access to these information resources.

Library workers should use professional judgement when conducting themselves in public, which extends to social media use. They are encouraged to throw out their bias or personal grudgewhen evaluating social media contents. It is natural for personal bias to be interlinked with the creative work that is produced on a professional level. So, it is important to seek multiple perspective and objective feedback to ensure inclusivity with the library's media environment.

The American Library Association has adopted the Library Bill of Rights to provide library governing authorities,librarians, other library staff, and library users with guidelines on theconstitutional principles applied to the U.S. Libraries. This document provides a policy and implementation framework for public and academic libraries engaging in the use of social media. The following information is provided solely as a guideline for creating a social media policy and is not intended to as a comprehensive list of requirements or legal advice.

Libraries are under no legal obligation to participate in social media, nor are they required to host a public conversation. A library could choose, for instance, to solely participate in one way communication, that is, to make announcements and seek or respond to questions or comments. But once a Public Library or publicly funded Academic Library does invite conversation, it may be considered to have established a designated public forum.

To avoid having a library's platform hijacked by content unrelated to the library mission (including commercial or simply irrelevant speech), libraries should carefully and narrowly craft their public declarations of purpose and acceptable behaviour as tied to the mission of the library. Not all issues apply to every library, but omissions and additions can be made based on the library's individual needs. Adopting the best practices, a library's social media policy should consider the following issues:

Purpose and Scope: The library should make its social media policy publicly available on its website. There is a range of possible community engagement levels available to libraries. Some examples are listed below:

a. The library posts information related to its services and does not seek out or respond to comments.

b. The library posts information and conducts occasional calls for survey responses or comments. The library reserves the right to close comments at a predetermined time, and it may not respond to the comments received.

c. The library invites people to post or comment occasionally on variousissues.

d. The library engages with its community regarding matters related to library resources and services.

e. The library serves as a forum for the discussion on many issues related to its collections and programmes.

f. Statements may also address the purpose ofthelibrary and its governing body such as "Our library's mission is to promote the value and importance of library services, programmes and collections."

Audience: As the best practice, the library should identify its intended audience. An Academic Library may limit its intended audience to university faculty, students, staff, administrators and alumni. It can be expanded further to include specialized communities outside the university, such as scholars within a particular discipline, or even the general public. Public Libraries may identify their audience as those people residing within their official service area.

Responsibility:All library staff responsible for contributions to library social media platforms should be thoroughly trained in not only best practices for individual social media platforms but in the mission, values, and positions of the library and its governing body to the parent institution. A social media account serves asthe digital face of the library. It should maintain the same level of customer service provided in the physical library. The library should outline appropriate staff behaviour and responsibilities in its social media entity. All staff should apply these guidelines in a consistent manner.

Staffcontributors should use a tone consistent with their organization's communication and marketing strategy, whether posting original content or communicating directly with a user. Be friendly, sincere, and energetic. Social media content should be written from the pointof view of the "We", which represents the library as a whole and not as an individual staff member. The online face of the library and staff members should remain professionalat all times. They should refrain from expressing their personal views when posting on the library's behalf.

Library staff should protect patron privacy and confidentiality whenever possible. Social media platforms should not be used to collect information about the library's users. Information shared by patrons on the library's social media should not be kept by the library to be used for other purposes. Staff should be trained and aware of basic cybersecurity practices. Librarians and library staff should refer to the committee on professional ethics.

Reconsideration: Social media policies should provide recourse for individuals to express complaints or concerns about the content posted on the library's social media. This establishes an objective and uniform framework for all involved while protecting the creative freedom and skills needed to engage library communities. The procedure for handling complaints and reconsidering social media contents should be clearly enunciated in the policy statement. The policy should be strict that no posts will be removed without following the approved procedure. No content should be removed upon the authority of a single staff member or administrator.

Acceptable Behaviour: Libraries should clearly state that their social media behaviour policy is prominently displayed on their website. A social media policy clearly defines acceptable and unacceptable behaviour. Unacceptable behaviour that may result in the removal of a post or the temporary blocking of a user could include speech that is not protected by the law such as copyright violations, obscenity,child pornography, defamatory or libellous comments,or threats against the library.

Library Staff or Other Users: As the best practice, policies should state that unprotected speech is not permitted as a facilitator of a public discussion. However, libraries should be aware that enforcement of such policies to ban unprotected speech could prove difficult as library staff would be put in the position of determining whether particular speech fits within the legal definition of the unprotected speech category.

In crafting their social media policies, libraries should be further aware that removing posts that do not fit within the definition of unprotected speech, may be offensive to other users.

A library can urge its users to adhere to the established and acceptable policies and to engage in civildiscourse.

Consequences: Libraries should clearly state the consequences for poststhat do not meet the library's social media policy. It should be drafted in consultation with legal counsel.

The social media content of a Public Library or publicly funded Academic Library can be subject to an open record. All users' posts that are removed for areason whatsoever should be securely retained in accordance withtheorganization's retention schedule. The policy for how long a library retains these social media posts should be clearly stated in the social media policy and reviewed by legal counsel.Library administrators should clearly communicate their social media policies and legal obligations to their vendors.

Disclaimer: Libraries should state that comments expressed on any social media platform do not reflectthe views or position of the library, its offices, or its employees. Social media users should exercise their own judgement about the quality and accuracy of any information presented through social media.

Additional Information: The staff of the office is available to answer questions to provide information to librarians, trustees, educators, and the public about social media policy and practice.

The Conclusion: The Intellectual Freedom Committee recommends that libraries should participate in social media after thoughtfully reviewing the guidelines presented,and adopt a social media policy in consultation with legal counsel that reflects their institution's intent and capacity. Social media presents an opportunity for libraries to engage with users and to make significant contributions to share knowledge. This robust civic engagement leads to an informed citizenry and a healthy society, and also demonstrating the great value of our institutions.

CHAPTER 15

FINANCIAL SOURCES OF LIBRARY

Whatever may there be the size and nature of a library, some sources of finance are common to all such asgrants from Government, library fee, donations, endowments, library tax, late fee, etc. Besides these, some miscellaneous sources are as under:

a. Sale proceeds of old magazines, paper and other items which are useless.
b. Fees charged for library publication.
c. Interest received on funds deposited in banks.
d. Funds raised by organizing fund-raising programmes, etc.
e. University libraries in India receive grants from boththe Central Government and the State Governments.

Some other sources of the library are as under:

Self-FinancialArrangement: University Grants Commission expects the universities for arranging their own finance. Education in India is a social welfare service.As such, it is endeavoured to provide education free of cost. This form of a library is changing slowly into the marketing of library services. Grant is the chief source of finance for the University Library.

The University Library receives a fixed amount from the annual budget of the university budget besides a grant from the state administration. University Library receives a fixed amount from the State Government and the Central Government. It is received on an annual basis or under the five-year plan. The grant by the Central Government is given through the University Grants Commission. The local administration gives an additional amount for the libraries. It is in addition to the grant given to the universities on an annual basis. The UGC gives the following types of grants to libraries:

Donations and Endowments: Income is received in the libraries in the form of donations and endowments alsofrom some international organizations. In this category come the following funds:

a. A special fund of the United Nations Organization
b. The fund of UNESCO.
c. The fund of Ford Foundation.

Trust: Libraries also receive a large amount from this source such as annual fee and fine for depositing the books after the due date. This type of income is very nominal.

Profit and Exchange: Income under this head is as follows:

a. Income from selling their own publications by libraries.
b. Money received by the libraries in the form of books and other literature received in exchange fortheir publications.
c. Library accepts nominal charges from the readers for issuing books to them or a deposit equal to the price of the book.

CHAPTER 16

LIBRARY LEGISLATION IN INDIA

Act means preparing the format of law or legislation. In the context of libraries, the Library Act means to give legal provision for establishing a library system,its maintenance, service, function, right and management under any state or a national government. Library legislation is capable of regulating various organs of public library services. It is an instrument for the development of the public in a uniform pattern. It can help in promoting a sense of self-consciousness among the people who would feel it obligatory on their part to use services offered by the library.

In the year 1850, the first Library Act was passed in Great Britain. The Kolhapur Public Libraries Act (1949) was the first library act in India. It was followed by Andhra Pradesh in 1960, Karnataka 1965, Maharashtra 1967, West Bengal 1979, Manipur 1988, Kerala 1989, Mizoram 1993, and Goa in 1994. It was also followed by the Gujarat State in 2002 and Bihar state 2008. At present,most of the countries specify free use of public library services.

Need for Library Legislation: Provision of public library services is a natural corollary to the democratic way of life. Free communication is essential for the preservation of a free society for the utilization of services. It has been experienced that public library services can be effectively offered only through legislation. Library legislation is needed for the reasons mentioned below:

1. It helps in creating necessary conditions under which public libraries can be established nationwide.
2. To put the Public Library on a sound and sure financial footing by way of levy of library tax.
3. To make the Public Library dependent on subscription, donation or private gift and to save the library from political

influence.

4. For creating a sound administrative setup.To provide permanent, efficient, balanced and coordinated library services and also for proper lineof growth.
5. To solve the problem of land, building, legacies, etc.
6. For centralized services like acquisition, processing, etc.

The library legislation has the provision of financial support to the public libraries. But the provision to be made in library legislation would depend upon the social, political and economic environment.

CHAPTER 17

LIBRARY LEGISLATION: NECESSITY AND IMPORTANCE

LIBRARY LEGISLATION: It is universally accepted that public library service isa social liability of the Government. If there is a legal sanction, the results are better. At present, we notice remarkable changes in library services. These changes are as a result of the enforcement of Library Acts. In the countries, where the Library Acts are proved effective, the citizens enjoy library services of the highest order. Due to the Library Act, the nation becomes entitled to raise money in the form of surcharge for the library services.

DEFINITION: Library Act has been defined by DrVibhasi as "A Law or Act passed by the competent authority of the nation or State which provides a scientific basis for the establishment of the libraries, safety of the collected study material, its unhindered use and its services." Its objectives are as under:

a. To utilize the material collected in the subordinate libraries.
b. To keep safely all the materials.
c. To develop the libraries.
d. To keep the continuity of the library services.

IMPORTANCE OF LIBRARY LEGISLATION: The importance of library service lies in the fact that with its help, masses may be educated, and national, political and educative consciousness or awareness may be assured. This is the reason why the Library Advisory Committee laid emphasis on strengthened library service in its report. It held that there is an acute necessity to get the Public Library Acts passed by the States at the earliest. Dr Ranganathan clearly held that the library services should be provided by Statutory Act for the welfare of the State. We have the necessity of the Public Library Act at National and State level as under:

Legal Protection: This is the social duty of the Government to organize the public library service at the National and State level. If there is some legal or statutory force behind it, the services are rendered in a more satisfactory way. In the past, there was a lack of legal protection. As a result, the working system of the libraries lacked uniformity. Simultaneously, there was a scarcity of finance. The Library Act solves all the problems that are parts of public administration. For example- land, building, finance, sale, purchase of property for the library, etc. S. Dasgupta has highlighted the importance of the Library Act in his book "Library Development." He has enumerated its importance as under:

The Act determines the structure. It determines the development within an ideal outline. It checks the disordered, unnecessary as well as undesirable development that takes place on the imagination or whims of the politicians and administrators. The Act determines a proper authority for the administration of the libraries. It ascertains that the library authority should be organized in such a way as it may be responsible for making a law influential.The Act makes provision for permanent and gradual financial aid. Advantages of legal protection are as under:

i.   Dispute, if any, may be solved on the basis of legal protection.
ii.   The control of administration is exercised over service rendered.
iii. The library services are rendered smoothly.
iv.   It brings in uniformity in the library service.
v.   It strengthens the financial position. Thedevelopment of the public library's services needs strong finance. The most effective means for finance is library tax. But it cannot be imposed without Act. The Library Advisory Committee has requested the State Government to pass Library Acts. The Committee was of the opinion that library tax might be

imposed only through legislation. The reason is that no tax can be imposed unless sanctioned by law. There may be two methods:

a. The Municipal Act may be amended, and library tax may be imposed, and

b. A nationwide Library Act may be enacted authorising the State Government and local bodies to charge library tax. In this way, it is clear that the strong financial position is the pivot, around which the wheels of libraries development may revolve.

i. It brings improvement in the position. At present, most of the libraries are in a pitiable condition. For want of space, collection and finance, they have to confine themselves to the task of issuing and receiving back the study material. Due to the financial crisis, they are unable to purchase new books. As a result, people are indifferent to the Public Libraries. It is essential to pass the Act to bring improvement in the present position of the public library service.

ii. The Act appoints an administrative unit for every unit of the library service. In this way, the administrative unit conducts and controls the function or working of every unit of library service

The assumption is that library services should be provided free of cost to all the people. Charges received from the readers for using the library services cannot be sufficient to bear the library services. There will be a fall in the number of its users if charges are increased irrationally. As a result, there would be no proper use of the library. Hence, financial aid and grants from the Government to the library is essential. A library may be a regular recipient of the grant from the Government only if there is an Act.

CHAPTER 18

DELIVERY OF BOOKS ACT

Delivery of Books Act, 1954: The Act was passed on 20 May 1954. The Act provides for the delivery of books to the National Library and other Public Libraries. This Act may be called the Delivery of Books (Public Libraries) act, 1954. It extends to the whole of India except the State of Jammu and Kashmir. In this Act, Public Library means the National Library at Calcutta and any three other Libraries which may be specified by the Central Government in this behalf bythe notification in the Official Gazette.

Under this Act, book includes every volume, part or division of a volume or pamphlet, in any language, and every sheet of map, chart or plan separately printed or lithographed, but does not include, a newspaper published in conformity with the provision of Section 5 of the Press and Registration of Books Act, 1867.

Delivery of Books to Public Library: According to Press and Registration of Books Act, 1867, the publisher of every book, published in the territories to which this Act extends, shall deliver at his own expense a copy of the books to the National Library at Calcutta and one such copy to each of the other three Public Libraries within thirty days from the date of its publication.

The copy delivered to the National Library shall be a copy of the whole book with all maps and illustrations belonging thereto finished and clouded in the same manner as the best copies at the same, and shall be bound, sewed or stitched together and on the best paper on which any copy of the book is printed.

The copy delivered to any other Public Library shall be on the paper on which the largest number of copies of the books is printed for sale, and shall be in the like condition as the book prepared for sale.

Receipt of Books Delivered: The Person-in-Charge of a Public Library (whether called librarian or by any other name) or any other person authorised by him in his behalf to whom a copy of a book is delivered shall give to the publisher a receipt in writing therefor.

Penalty: Any publisher who contravenes any provision of this Act or any rule made thereunder shall be punishable with a fine of rupees or by other ways decided by the Court.

Cognizance of Offence: No Court shall take cognizance of any offence punishable under this Acttosave on complaint made by an officer empowered in this behalf by the Central Government by a General or special order.

No Court inferior to that of a Presidency Magistrate or a Magistrate of the first class shall try any offence punishable under this Act.

The Act shall also apply to books published by or under the authority of the Government other than books meant for official use only.

The Central Government may, by notification in the Official Gazette, make rules to carry out the purposes of this Act.

At present, nearly all the States have enacted such laws whereunder the publishers are obliged to send one or more copies of each published book to the administration or prescribed libraries free of cost. This law is needed for the following reasons:

1. We need to have knowledge of the culture and civilization of the country. If the copies of the books are available in the library, the readers go through them and come to know about the country's culture and civilization.

2. We need legal aid. On so many times, the topics discussed in the books become disputed. To settle these disputes, the production of such books before the court is essential. If the books are available with the Government, they may be produced in the Courtsoon.

3. We need this Act for the development of our knowledge. To

facilitate the systematic development of knowledge, it is essential that the studies made by scholars should be available to readers. To enable the readers, keeping a copy of the book is necessary.

4. To fulfil the above objects, the Government under the "Delivery of Books Act" instructs every publisher to send one copy of each published book.

In India, Press and Registration Act was passed in 1867. According to this Act, two copies of every book in the county will be forwardedtothe Government of India through the District Magistrate. Copies received as above by the Government of India are kept intheNational Library, Belvedere, Calcutta.

In 1954, the Government of India passed the "Delivery of Books Act". In 1956,thenecessary amendment was made to this law. It was provided that every publisher would forward one copy of every book published to the undermentioned libraries within a period of thirty days of their publication:

   i.   National Library, Calcutta.
  ii.   Asiatic Society Library, Bombay.
 iii.   Connemara Public Library, Madras.
  iv.   Delhi Public Library, Delhi.

In this way, the above four main libraries got the right of getting one copy each of every book published by every publisher in the country.

CHAPTER 19

COPYRIGHT LAWS

Copyright Laws protect Expression of Ideas rather than the ideas themselves under section 13 of the Copyright Act, 1957. Copyright protection is conferred on literary works, dramatic works, musical works, artistic works, cinematography, films and sound recording. Copyright is a form of intellectual property protection granted under Indian law. The creators of original literary works including computer programmes, tables, compilations,computer databases, dramatic, musical or artistic works, cinematographic films and sound recordings are protected under this Act.

Copyright refers to a bundle of exclusive rights vested in the owner of copyright by virtue of Section 14 of the Act. These rights can be exercised only by the owner of the copyright or by any other person who is duly licensed in this regard by the owner of the copyright. These rights include the right of adoption, right of reproduction, right of publication, right to make translation and right to make communication to the public.

Copyright protection is conferred to all original literary, artistic, musical, dramatic or cinematographic works. Original means that the work has not been copied from any other source. Copyright protection commences the moment a work is created. Its registration is optional. However, it is always advisable to obtain a registration for better protection. Copyright registration does not confer any right and is merely a prima facie proof of an entity in respect of the work in the copyright register maintained by the Registrar of Copyright.

As per section 17 of the Act, the author or creator of the work isthe first owner of the copyright. An exception to this rule is that the employer becomes the owner of the copyright in circumstances where the employee creates a work in the course and scope of employment.

Copyright registration is invaluable to acopyright holder who wishes to take civil or criminal action against the infringer. Registration formalities are simple, and the paperwork is easy. In case, the work has been created by a person other than an employee; it would be necessary to file with the application a copy of the assignment deed.

The Copyright Act, 1957 provides copyright protection in India. It confers copyright protection to the author of paintings, sculpture, and drawing or of the manuscript of a literary,dramatic or musical work. If he is the first owner of the copyright,heshall be entitled to have a right to share in the resale price of such original copy provided that the resale price exceeds rupees ten.

Copyright means the monopoly of the writer on his works. Copyright also means the right of Government to get one or more copies of each printed books. It includes also the right of library determined by the Government to get the above-said copies.

According to copyright, the writer has the following rights:

   i.   To publish the book or to change it in any material form.
   ii.   To copy the content.
  iii.   To present the whole extract publically.
   iv.   To publish his manuscript.
   v.   To get the translation of the printed work published.

In this way, it is clear that the writer reserves his right legally- the right to express his language, style, original thoughts, etc. in any way. Hecandelegate his copyright willingly in writing to the publisher or any otherperson. The information about the person recipient of the right is printed behind the title cover with the mark alongwith name and year.

On the basis of the copyright, the writer does not lose his right over the content even after the book has been published. He continues to have his right over the language andstyle. The other persons have to obtain his permission before using his thoughts in his language and style. This permission is granted in two forms:

i.   If only a few extracts of the letter are to be taken and used in another book, the extracts are presented with the writer's name. For example- according to the author, namely...

ii. If much of the matter from the book is to be taken, the permission from the writer is to be obtained in writing.

In this way, the copyright means to keep the right of the author over the book reserved.

Infringement of Copyright: A copyright owner cannot enjoy his right unless the infringement of the same is stringently dealt with by the Courts. The approach of the Indian Judiciary in this regard is very satisfactory.

A Person who innocently or even accidentally infringes other's copyright may be held liable under the Copyright Act of the US and under the laws of various other countries. The guilty intention of the offender can be taken into account for determining the quantum of damage to be awarded for the alleged infringement.

CHAPTER 20

LIBRARY RULES

The library rules are formed by the executive committee or administrative body of the library. Rules are necessary forthelibrary to avoid the chances of misuse and misconduct. The rules are formed for the readers of the library. The library services are conducted according to these rules. The library personnel bear the responsibility to ensure that these rules are followed by all the persons affected. The library rules must be formed on a legal basis so that legal advice can be taken in case the rules are infringed.

Need of Rules: We need library rules to protect the reading material and to prevent damaging other property of the library. We need it to prevent mismanagement in the library and to facilitate the proper use of library services. To make the readers and the employees of the library aware of their duties and responsibilities, we need them much. We need library rules at the most to resolve any dispute arising out of any situation in the library.

Library rules are needed for fulfilment of library objectives and providing certain guidelines to the library personnel and readers. To regulate the working hours of the library, its membership and terms and conditions of charging and discharging books, library rules are needed. We need it more essentially to inflict punishment to members who hinder the smooth functioning of the library. General rules of a decent library are as under:

a. An identity card is compulsory for getting access to the library.
b. Silence is to be maintained.
c. No discussion permitted inside the library.
d. Registration should be done to become a library member prior to using the library resources.

   e. No personal belongings allowed inside the library.

   f. Textbooks, printed material and issued books are not allowed to be taken inside the library.

   g. Using mobile phones and audio instruments with or without speaker or headphone isstrictly prohibited in the library premises.

   h. Enter your name and sign in the register kept at the entrance counter before entering the library.

   i. Show the books and other materials which are being taken out of the library to the staff at the exit counter.

   j. The library may recall any book from any member at any time, and the member shall return the same immediately.

   k. Library borrower cards are not transferable. The borrower is responsible for the books borrowed on his card.

   l. Refreshment of any kind shall not be taken anywhere on the library premises.

   m. Admission of students to the library is allowed only on the production of their valid identity cards.

Issues System: Books will be issued on the presentation ofalibrary card along with the identity card. Students are instructed to check the book while borrowing, and they will be responsible for any type of damage or mutilation noticed at the time of return.

Overdue Charges: Materials borrowed should be returned on or before the due date stamped. If returned late, the overdue fine will be charged for the delayed period.

Books Lost: If the books are lost, the borrower shall replace the books of the same edition or latest edition or pay double cost of the book after getting permission from the librarian.

Take special care to maintain the library borrower cards. Do not fold and do not alter the entries made on the cards. Members are responsible for the entire set of library borrower cards issued to them.

Loss of card should be reported to the librarian. The duplicate card may be issued against formal application and fine.

The Validity of Cards: Library borrower cards are valid for the entire duration of the course to access library facilities. At the end of the course, borrower cards shall be returned to the library.

No Dues Certificate: Each student shall obtain "No Dues Certificate" from the library after returning all the books issued, surrendering the borrowers' card and after paying outstanding dues if any.

Care of Library Books: Students are required to handle the books and journals very carefully. Marking with pencil, writing or highlighting, tearing the pages or mutilating the same in any other way will be viewed seriously. In such a case,thereader shallbe held responsible unless these are brought to the notice of the library staff at the time of receipt of the book.

Different Library Rules: Different library rules are formed for different types of libraries. These rules are formed according to the nature of each library.Rules for a particular library cannot work in another library. To illustrate, the rules formed for an Educational Library cannot be applicable to Public Library. In the same way, the rules of Public Library cannot work in a College or University Library. However, certain types of rules may be common to all libraries. Such common rules are as under:

a. Rules related to the general operation of the library.
b. Rules related to issue and receipt of books.
c. Rules regarding charging of a fee for late deposit of borrowed books.
d. Rules to prevent misuse of the library property.
e. Rules for increasing the use of the Library.

Rules for Working Hours and Holidays: It is essential to fix the view of the needs and convenience of its readers. These rules should be formed on the basis of the first law of library science, implying "Books are for Use." Hence, the following points should be kept in view:

a. Adjustment: Working hours of the library can be adjusted according to the local climatic conditions.

b. Maximum Working Hours: The library should remain open for a maximum time.

c. Minimum Holidays: The holidays should be limited to any important national events and religious festivals.

d. Discontinuance well in Time: The charging-discharging of books should be discontinued well before the closing hours of the library. It would enable the employees to get sufficient time for completion of the daily activities and preparing for the activities of the next day.

Rules Relating to Admission: Admission to the library should remain open to all, even if they are not members of the library. This is necessary because many persons may be interested in visiting the library, although they are not members of the library. In this connection, some rules should be as under:

a. Anti-social elements, alcoholics or those persons who are suffering from some contagious disease or infection, etc. should not be allowed to enter the library. The reason is that their admission is harmful to other visitors.

b. The person who enters the library must be made to enter his full name, address and signature in registerconcerned kept at the library entrance.The reason behind is evidence that he has accepted to follow all rules and regulations of the library.

c. Readers should not be allowed to bring pets or personal belongings in the library.

Rules Relating to Membership: Main rules relating to membership should be as under:

> The rules determining the membership of the library should be liberal. It would result in an increase in membership. The rules should be such as to enable every person in the locality to become a member of the library. No charges in the form of membership fees etc. should be taken from the readers. It would discourage membership. Recommendation of some reputed person in the area can be taken at the time of registration. It would be proof of the applicant being a bonafideperson.The name and address of the reader should be attested in this recommendation letter.

Rules for Library Services: Rules relating to the use of library services should be simple and clear. There should be no ambiguity. Rules should be clear to determine the type of readers that will be allowed to loan the books from the library. Rules are needed to determine how the readers can use the reference books or other such books and periodicals that cannot be taken out of the library. Rules are needed to fix a limit on the number of days for which the readers can keep the books so that the maximum number of readers can keep the books and use them. It is suggested that the time duration should be different for different types of readers. Some suggestions are as under:

a. It can be 15 days for students,
b. 30 days for researchers, and
c. 90 days for professors.

Before re-issuing a book to the same reader, it should be confirmed that no other reader has made any reservation or request for the particular book. There should be rules for charging late fees if the readers do not return the books within the stipulated time. There should be clear rules regarding the loan of books. Books should be loaned to the readers only when they present their membership letter with the Reader's Ticket. The number of books loaned to a reader should not be more than the number of books sanctioned and written on the Reader's Ticket. All liability of misuse of the Reader's Ticket, if it is lost, should be put on the reader. A duplicate Reader's Ticket should be issued only after taking appropriate charges for it. The reader should be asked to submit an indemnity bond. There should be rules pertaining to the Reservation of Books.

Rules Relating to Restricted Reading Material: Clear and specific rules should be framed restricting the loan of such types of books to the readers:

Rare books, very expensive books, illustrative books, books that are very large in size, manuscripts, periodicals and other books that are very much in demand by the readers.

Rules Relating to Ban on Misuse: The gate-keeper should check the books and other reading material loaned to the readers at the library gate. A reader should not be allowed to carry the book outside the library premises without getting them issued in a proper way. There should be rules to punish those readers who commit to tear or remove the pictures, charts, photographs and other pages from the books or damage the books by writing on the pages or by any means. It is necessary to charge such readers the full cost of the damaged books. There should be rules to give strict punishment to readers who damage or mutilate the library property in any way. The rules should authorise the librarian to impose pecuniary or monetary punishment on such readers or to cancel their membership.

Rules Relating to Disobedience: There may be some readers who do not follow the above rules or disobey the rules of the library. There should be a rule of library authorising the librarian to restrict the readers who disobey the rules of library services without giving any reason. Their membership may even be terminated or suspended for some time in the form of punishment. Readers who are reckless or wilfully late in returning the books should also be punished in the like manner.

The librarian bears the responsibility of ensuring that the rules of the library are followed and obeyed by its members. Therefore, certain rights and powers should be given to the librarian empowering him to take action against anti-social elements to punish the miscreants in the library to prohibit such members who soil the library premises, disturb other readers, smoke in library premises, sleep in the reading rooms, etc.

CHAPTER 21

REPROGRAPHY

Reprography is a science and practice of copying and reproducing documents and graphic material. It is the reproduction of graphics through mechanical or electrical means such as photography or xerography. Reprography is commonly used in catalogues and archives as well as in the architectural,engineering, and construction industries. Reprography is a form of reproduction, i.e. the duplication of work.

When we use the quotes and views of other writers in our own words with reference to making our own views authentic, the work is called reprography. To bring into light the hidden knowledge and publish new books without studying several books published earlier is not possible. Hence, reprography is made. It has the approval of the law in the copyright. It is all fair in the book writing process. It has the recognition and concurrence of the scholarly world recognised in the form of "Fair Use."

"Fair Use" of reprography is the necessity of copyright. Under the provisions of this law, it is held that reprography without permission of the copyright holder is legal. However, there is a condition regarding reprography under "Fair Use"that the matter should not be used for exclusive commercial purpose.

Reprography is used by the research scholars pursuing special and higher studies. It is used by scholars who write their thesis and articles. In the higher educational circle, the Ph.D. degree has become essential. Hence, reprography is being used more and more.

a. In reprography, the libraries get a prescribed form filled up by the readers. In the form, it is clearly mentioned that the matter will not be misused by him. These days, the use of reprography has increased and deeply affected the copyright. However, it is highly acceptable.

CHAPTER 22

ESSENTIALS OF LIBRARY SCIENCE

Read the Books at the Most: The first principle of library science is that we should use our library at the most. Newton's first rule of motion states: "If a thing is static, it will continue to be static until some external force is applied to it to change this state." At present, the librarian acts upon this law sincerely. He is overjoyed when he sees the books being issuedtothereaders rapidly and continuously to make this law effective. Attention is paid to the undermentioned things:

Easy Access Location: For the fullest use of the library, the first condition is its location. It should be located at easy access. It should be established at such a place where the maximum numbers of users may reach easily and conveniently. If it is possible, the library should be located in the heart of the city. Besides, there should be proper arrangement of convenience to reach the library. Only in that position, more and more users of the library will be benefitted.

Reading Hours: The opening time and closing time of the library should be according to the convenience of the users. If this period is not in their accordance, the library material will not be of much use. On the contrary, if the working hours of the library are such as the common users may go there after performing their usual functions and activities conveniently, the library material will be used to its maximum.

Essentials of Library Hall: A good library has main necessities as under:

The library building should be attractive and clean. Proper arrangement of light and air should be there in the building. Almirah should be near the entrance where new books may be displayed. There should be sufficient space for various departments. There should be proper provision for accommodation for various activities, e.g. debate, discussion, lecture, reading room, open shelves, etc. The equipment in the library playsamajor role in the use of the library. Hence, some suggestions are as under:

a. Racks and almirahs should be conveniently kept for the users.
b. Their colour and structure should be attractive.
c. Height of shelves should not be too much. Normally, it should be seven feet high.
d. Other equipmentlike tables, stools, chairs, etc. should be according to Indian Standard Institute approved the standard.

a. Card-holders and counters should be attractive.
b. It should be well-furnished.

If the above conditions are fulfilled, the users would like to stay in the library for more time and make the maximum utilization of the library.

Open Access: Open access should be adopted to enhance the use of the library. It will facilitate readers' effort to obtain the books needed by them.

Library Rules: The library rules should be simple. They should be framed keeping in view the convenience of the reader. Rules should be flexible so that they may be modified to meet the need of the time.It is necessary for the maximum use of the library that the staff members should be trained, efficient, diligent and talented. They should have the following virtues:

The staff members of a library should have the knowledge of what is consistent with the study material kept in the library. If a reader approaches them and asks for particular information, they should be able to tell readily which book, magazine or any other material would be available.

They should have the capacity of helping the readers in utilizing the study material. They should have requisite academic and professional qualifications. Their rank and salary should be equal to the employees having the same qualifications and rendering a similar type of service in the Department.

They should be sincere in their duties. The employees should be diligent, polite and submissive. Such employees may be called the assets of the library. Such an employee with his amicable behaviour and service attitude cooperates the readers in selecting the required books and encourages them to visit frequently.

The utility of a library consists of its frequent use by a great number of readers. If the books are not selected and procured according to the necessity, standard, taste and interest of the readers, they will avoid visiting the library. In that position, its purpose will be defeated.

Every reader should get his book. A few centuries ago, it was considered that the books were for a few distinguished or privileged persons only. But nowadays the modern libraries entitle all the classes of society to make healthy use of the collection in the library. Individual, society and nation will make progress only if the library is made for public use. In this way, this rule puts emphasis on the principle that the entrance to education and knowledge should be open to all.

Now the question is- who should bear the liability of making books available to every person? This liability is not on the shoulders of any one person but onthe shoulders of all the people. A library can be successful only if State, Library Committee, Readers' Community and Library Staff perform respective duties sincerely keeping in view the points below:

Every Book Gets Its Reader: The emphasis is put on the availability of able reader for every book. Every sort ofliteratureavailable in the library should be properly utilized by the readers. These days, literature is being published at a rapid pace, and to make it available to the reader is a significantwork.To materialize this purpose, the library issues directions to put the following methods into practice:

Systematic Books Arrangement: If the books are arranged properly on the shelves, it becomes easy for every book to find its readers. The books are arranged on the shelves according to some standard and recognised classification method. If the books on a subject and allied subjects are kept together in a classified order, the attention of the reader is automatically attracted towards all the books available on that subject in the library.

Easy Access: In the library, books should be easily accessible to readers. Students are extended liberty to a certain limit to see and go through the book. They are granted permission to go to the almirahs and shelves without any obstruction. They are free to choose the books needed. When the readers are making a search ofthe books required by them,they get a chance to see and turn the pages of other books kept on the same shelves. In such a situation,every book gets a chance to have its readers. The open shelf system facilitates the use of the books and increases the chance for every book to get its reader.

Books Selection:If the books are selected and procured according to the necessities, tastes and demands of the reader;every book will get its readers.

Books Catalogue: Library catalogue is prepared to furnish full information to the readers about the study material present in the library.The catalogue renders a great help to every book in finding its reader. The catalogue should be complete, exhaustive, scientific and up-to-date. It should include series entry, analytical entry, cross-reference entry, cross reference index entry, etc. These entries render help to every book in getting its readers.

Books Exhibition: It is human nature to attract to a new thing.Books in the exhibition attract every person who looks at it. Hence, the newly purchased books should be displayed on the shelves meant for them. These shelves should be along the entrance so that every reader who passes by may catch a glimpse of them. In such a position, the reader would certainly observe the books, turn their pages, and if be interesting and serving his purpose, read one of them.

Referential Purpose: Readers are often in need of information. They often go to the library to meet their necessity. They are given this help by the Reference Section. The Reference Section of a library establishes personal relationships with the readers who go to consult the section.

Special Display of Books: Some books, although useful, happen to lie in the library without catching the attention of the reader. To bring such books into the light and have readers for them, it is essential to arrange for their special display. It will facilitate the availability of reader for those books.

Time-Saving: The library staff should save the time of the reader from the moment he steps in the library until he gets the required information or reaches the proper book. The staff member should provide him with prompt services and save his valuable time. It is emphasized that reforms should be brought in the library and it's running with a view to providing the readers with more and more facility.

ShelfArrangement: Makinga proper arrangement of books on the shelves also is an effective factor. This work should be done subject-wise, and by recognised classification method. The arrangement may be as under:

a. The books in great use should be arranged in the beginning.
b. The reference books should be arranged near the counter.
c. Proper arrangement for guides should be made at the entrance or the stock-room. From these guides, the readers will come to know about the arrangement of the study material. In this way, the valuable time of readers can be saved.
d. The library catalogue should be made on a scientific basis. It should be exhaustive and up-to-date. Such a catalogue saves

the time of the readers as well as staff members. The catalogue can be made for the readers with such columns- Writer, Subject, Text, Translator, Editor, Artist, Book-Series, Publisher, etc.

Circulation: The process of arrival and exit of the books is called circulation. This work should be done on a scientific basis. It is done sothatthe time of the readers, as well as staff members, can be saved. The traditional register system takes too much time. Hence, a simple and scientific method should be applied in its place. In the modern libraries, card and mechanical circulation technique are used.

Growth is the size of the Library. The increase in the size of the library indicates the growth of the library. In other words, it increases in the books, readers, number of staff members and its services.In view of the imminent increase, the library should be organized in such a way as the growth of the library should not suffer for want of building and other facilities.

After a library is fully developed, it is essential to have control over the increase of the books. Keeping this point in view, unuseful books should be weeded out, and development should be maintained.

CHAPTER 23

LIBRARY DISPLAY

The display is an act in which books and other reading material are openly displayed for catching the attraction of the readers. In-library display, books lying unused for a long time are introduced to the readers and newcomers. The books and periodicals are presented for the benefit of the readers. Library display aims at introducing the new reading material to the readers.

The success of the library lies in the maximum use of its reading material. The library is a social institution that is used by the members of the public. In-library, classification and cataloguing are performed. They aim at giving information about the services offered by the libraries to the readers.

Importance of the library display is increasing day in day out. It is not possible for the readers to have and read the entire list of books and reading the material available on a specific subject. In this context, library display comes to an end and proves to be of great importance.

Purpose of Display: Main purpose of library display is to popularise the library. The display is a good means of contacting the general public. If the library display is done with great alertness and care, it can increase the popularity of the library to the desired level. A great benefit of the device is that no additional funds are needed for organizing the library display. But we have to take some precautions. First, we should use the funds available judiciously. Second, library personnel should be carefully utilized. If this is done, the display will add to the popularity of the library as well as increase the prestige of the library.

Library display increases interest in readers. It motivates people to read more books. It introduces all the books and reading material present in library collection to the general public. The readers are given information about the books of their interest.

Library display is a means of education. It is organized for educational purposes. It works as a bridge between the readers and new areas of knowledge. The information should be presented in such a manner as the readers can understand the contents of the reading matter. Library display gives information to the readers about the collection of books in the library and reading material received in the library. The library display can prove to be a very effective medium of education. Library display helps the librarian in performing his function. It helps the creation of an interesting atmosphere in cultural functions on special occasions. It helps scholars in their work in specific areas of education. It enhances the relation of the library with the public.

CHAPTER 24

PRINCIPLES OF LIBRARY MANAGEMENT

There has been a change in the principles according to the circumstances. Some principles have proved successful. The scholars and administrators have given them recognition. These principles are as under:

Single Window Command: It means that an employee should receive all the orders from a single authority. If it is so, the employee remains responsible for one person only. In case, there is a lack of unity of command; there remains an imminent possibility of indiscipline. The advantages of this system are that it becomes possible that activities would take place successfully. All staff members are expected to be in discipline.

Leadership: The basis of successful execution of all the principles is the leadership of the institution or organization. A member of the organization can give cooperation to the organization only when the Head of Institution is efficient, adept and of extraordinary intellectual and mental standard. Leadership has a quite wide meaning. It has the following functions:

a. To inspire other
b. To give guidance
c. To issue instruction and
d. To control them.

The librarian should be experienced, able and dynamic. He must possess courage, power of imagination, personality and physical capacity. The Library-in-Charge should be entitled to issue orders and instructions. In a big University Library, the In-Charge of every Department should be an Assistant Librarian. The Assistant Librarian should issue instructions to the subordinate staff. The Assistant Librarian should be given instructions by Additional Librarian or Deputy Librarian. The Librarian should issue instructions to the

Deputy Librarian. In such a working scenario, the staff would feel convenience in carrying out orders. And, there would be successful working in the library.

Managerial Unity: To keep up the unity of command, the managerial unity is essential in the institution. Some suggestions in this connection are as under:

a. There would be only one Head Librarian in the library.
b. There should be an officer in each library department for inspection.
c. Every department should have its own longing for the execution of objectives.
d. Execution should be looked after and controlled by an officer. The unity of management is needed for the scientific performance of the functions in the library.

Line and Length: Every work of the institution is done under the order and with advice. Orders are issued by the authority. On the other hand, the advisory work is done by staff members. In the absence of advice, the manager cannot perform any of his functions properly. The Head Librarian is empowered to take the advice of his Deputy Librarian on any special issue. The advisor may issue orders or instructions to the subordinate staff. The subordinate staff should be allowed to have initiative.For this purpose, the proper arrangement for advice and adjustment is essential.

System of Contact: This principle is concerned with the system of contact from the highest officer to the lowest officer. This principle holds that the employees must get orders through proper channel. The hierarchy is established like this- Head Librarian, Deputy Librarian, Assistant Librarian, Senior Technical Assistant, Junior Technical Assistant, etc. This is a scalar chain of officials. The officer of every level works under the officer of a higher level. The supervision and control of the work are also carried out in the same order.

Principle of Control: The assumption of this principle is that every officer and In-Charge should have under him only limited department or section and staff. In that position, the function of supervision and control can be performed properly.

Principle of Division of Labour: The assumption of this principle is that the Chief Officer or Authority should not confine to himself all the administrative functions and rights. Instead, he should delegate them to lower officials. This principle can be put to practice in a library on the basis of its size.

Departmentalization: All the functions of the institutions are divided in the form of departments, sections and groups, etc. Departmentalization is done mainly on the basis of physical forms of the matter such as works, subject, consumers and geographical situation.

Authority and Responsibility: It is universally known that authority and responsibility go together, when a managing authority is entrusted with some change of burden, he is given necessary rights so that he may carry out the work entrusted to him. The Chief Librarian should see whether various In-Charges of the Departments are utilizing their rights and doing their duties properly or not. The responsibility of the organization and management of the library should be on the Chief Librarian.

Principle of Standardization: This standardization is based on scientific management. Its object consists of uniformity and economy. The Indian Standard Institute is working in New Delhi. The ISI has fixed many standards. It is essential to manage according to these standards.

Mechanization: This principle can be called the principle of uniformity, economy and production increase. In this work, such things are necessary- uniformity, wide utility of the goods, economy and more work. For the smooth functioning of the library, it should be mechanized with equipment like computer, photostat machine and networks. All of this equipment enhances the working capacity.

Order: The word "Order" is a wide term. This term includes both the material and the staff. A nice system is needed for the efficient and effective performance of a function. If all the connected equipment, means, and persons occupy their proper place, the work is done specifically and economically. It is necessary that the library should be arranged on the basis of mutual relationships among functions.

Centralization and Decentralization: The policy of centralization and decentralization should be adapted to perform the institution's work efficiently and economically. There should be centralization for similar acts. Likewise, there should be decentralization for the convenience of the consumers. In the libraries, the centralization and decentralization are based on the various kinds of books. Centralization is a technical work and collection of study material is feasible and desirable.

Principle Regarding Personnel: This principle consists of the following up of discipline. Discipline means to have faith in the rules, to abide by the rules and to have respect for the concerned officers. To maintain discipline is essential in every institution. Only a good and able leader or Head can maintain nice discipline. In other words, keeping employees disciplined depends on the managers' personality.

Facility: There should be facilities for the employees. They must get the opportunity to take his problem to the highest authority and to see him. For this purpose, from time to time, meetings should be arranged so that the problems of the employees may be discussed and a proper decision to be taken.

Equality: It is essential to have friendly, just and liberal feelings with the employees. There should be an equal pay scale for equal work on the basis of activity and experience. Promotion should be on a seniority basis. No partiality should be observed with any employee. The feeling of equality insists dedication in the employees to work.

Permanency of Employee: Efficient administration is based on permanent personnel. Frequent change of the personal results in the failure of the management. Hence, it is essential to maintain stability in the tenure of employees so that the institution may develop.

Initiative: To take the initiative means that the manager and subordinate staff of every status should be permitted to give practical form to his process, method or experiments on the basis of his ability and efficiency. Independence instils enthusiasm in the employees to do more work. It results in the enhancement of their working capacity. Every administrator should give a chance to his subordinate for taking the initiative.

Pay Scale: In return of satisfactory work, there should be proper arrangement for the pay scale and increments according to the employee's ability and performance. It is essential to increase their ability and their sincere dutifulness.

Team Spirit: Organization is a strength. There should be a feeling of cooperation and unity in the employees. All the employees of the institution should work as a team. To enhance the feeling of cooperation, the manager would have to change his authoritative attitude. The manager should not say- "Do what I say." Instead, he should say- "Do what I do." He must adopt the policy of cooperation and participation.

Encouragement: The employees should be encouraged for doing more work satisfactorily. Some motivating elements should be present in the institution. They instil enthusiasm in the employees to do more and better. Theseelements may be powerful in such work- code of conduct, equality and team spirit, proper pay scale, bonus, necessary facilities, recognition, appreciation, reward, proper location, atmosphere, refresher course and training, chances of promotion, etc.

CHAPTER 25

LIBRARY COOPERATION

Cooperation means working together with somebody to achieve something.As for example- schools are working in close cooperation with parents to improve standards. Cooperation means any help that you give by doing what somebody asks you to do. As for example- the police asked the public for their cooperation in the investigation. The Hindi word for cooperation is "Sahakarita." It means to work together with a team spirit. In this way, it is clear that cooperation means the collective effort made to achieve common objectives. In cooperation, there is a feeling for all and all for one.

Various thinkers have defined the term cooperation in different ways. According to W. P. Wakins of International Cooperative Organization, "Cooperation is a technique of social organization. It is based on unity, economy, democracy, justice and liberty.

Cooperative is a voluntary organization of some individuals. This organization works for the interests of the whole community. It is a kind of social and economic organization. The basis of this cooperation is not profit.

In-library cooperation, some librarians Join together and work. Their objective is to utilize the study material available with them for the readers jointly. In case the libraries of a particular area or region work together, it will be called library cooperation. In-library cooperative, the libraries on the basis of mutual cooperation at the minimum possible charges make available the studymaterial to the maximum readers. In this way, the utilization of manpower, records, facilities, building, knowledge and equipment concerning library is called library cooperation.

Significance of LibraryCooperation: In the present times, there has been an unprecedented increase in the significance of education. With this increase, there has been an increase in the students, teachers and research scholars. The importance of library cooperation is as under:

After the invention of the printing press, there has been a rapid increase in the publication. In the presentworld,crores of books and magazines arealreadypublished. In such a position, it is impossible for any library to purchase and keep all the published books. In such a situation, library cooperation is a must.

By library cooperation, time and labour are saved. Overlapping can be avoided by doing the work on a collective basis. The same books need not be purchased in every library. The annual increase in the prices of the study material is from 10 to 20 per cent. On the contrary, the increase in thelibrary budget is only 5 to 10 per cent. Hence, the purchasing capacity of the libraries is decreasing gradually. The adjustment can be made on the basis of library cooperation.

Most of the libraries have limited sources of income. Hence, it is not possible for them to purchase all the books and magazines required and demanded by the readers. This shortage can be removed by books cooperation.

Every library cannot engage specialists for their services. The library cooperation makes the services of the specialists available to all the libraries. The library cooperation enables the readers of a country to have the knowledge of the research work carried out on other countries. This is of great importance.

In view of the space shortage in the libraries, books cooperation becomes necessary. New equipment like a photocopier, computers, etc. hasbecome necessary for the libraries. But all the libraries cannot procure such equipment due to their limited finance. Hence, there is the necessity of library cooperation. As regards the areas of library cooperation, it can be enumerated as under:

Acquisition: The libraries procure books, magazines and other study material from abroad also. In the process of acquisition, various works are done. For example-a selection of the books, placing orders, reminders, passing of bills and allied works are made. If these works are done on library cooperative basis, less expenditure would be incurred thereon.

Unified Cataloguing: In every library, the classification and cataloguing of the procured books is an important stage. If the work of classification and cataloguing is not done in separate places but in one place, there would be an economy. This is the reason why the National Library, Calcutta has the responsibility of classification and cataloguing function of all the books published all over the country.

Union Catalogue: The same catalogue of the books available in more than one library is called Union Catalogue. The catalogue is compiled and published separately on the basis of subject, language and study material. The preparation of the union catalogue of the books is exhaustive as well as expensive.

Exchange of Books: The exchange of study material available in various libraries has been a popular system. The inter-library exchange of books fulfils the objectives of the second and third laws of Library Science, i.e. every reader for every book, and every book for all readers.

Cooperative Storage: The problem of storage of space in libraries is becoming more and more critical in view of the rapidly increasing study material. Hence, it is necessary to remove unnecessary books regularly from the libraries. In this context, some suggestions are given below:

a. The catalogue of the unuseful books and magazines in the library should be published from time to time.
b. The catalogue should be forwarded to other libraries on a mutual loan basis. Every library preparessuch a catalogue and sends to the centre. The centre keeps the catalogues in circulation and arranges to send the books directly to the donor library.
c. Exchange of professional experts should be made. It would

be a nice thing to get in exchange for the specialists working in other developed libraries. These experts will be very useful in the underdeveloped libraries. They will contribute to the development of special works in newly born and underdeveloped libraries. They will make available new ways and practical knowledge of the technique to the staff working in these libraries.

d. Various kinds of ultra-modern equipment are being used in libraries.Among these, may be reckoned computer and reprographic appliances. In the present time, the help from the internet is proving more and more useful.

In this way, it is clear that by using the cooperation method in library equipment, it is possible to make the maximum use of the study material.

CHAPTER 26

LIBRARY PUBLIC RELATIONS

PUBLIC RELATIONS: According to the Oxford Advanced Learner's Dictionary, "Public relations is the business of giving the public information about a particular organization or person in order to create a good impression." For example, she works in public relations. The dictionary further says: "The state of the relationship between an organization and the public is public relations." The job of making a company, organization, etc. popular with the public is public relations.

Public relations is the practice of managing the speed of information between an individual or an organization and the public. Public relations may include an organization or individual gaining exposure to their audience using topics of public interest and news items that do not require direct payment.

Public relations is a strategic communication process that companies, individuals, and organizations use to build a mutually beneficial relationship with the public. Public relations professionals help a business or individual cultivate a positive reputation with the public through various unpaid or earned communications, including traditional media, social media, andpersonalengagements. They also help client defend their reputation during a crisis that threatens their credibility.

The Public Relations Society of America defines: "Public relations is a strategic communication process that builds mutually beneficial relationships between organizations and theirpublics."

Public relations is a management tool that is increasingly becoming important in the management of organization such as the library, whether private or public; whether they are profit-making or non-profit oriented. It is an essential element in all the communication system that enables individuals to be informed in many aspects of subjects that affects their lives.

Public relations is a distinctive management function which helps establish and maintainmutual lines of communication, understanding, acceptance and cooperation betweenanorganization and its publics. Public relation is an activity aimed at increasing communication and understanding between an organization and individual and one or more groups called public.

R. F.Harlow defines public relation like this: "Public relation is a science through which an organization can consciously attempt to fulfil its social responsibilities and to secure the public recognition and approval necessary to success."He also calls:"Public relations is the process whereby an organization analyses the needs and desires of all interested parties in order to conduct itself more responsively towards them."

Dimock says, "Public relations are concerned with survival because, in the long run, no enterprise can continue without public support."

Dr S. R Ranganathan says, "Well considered publicity is necessary forthe public library as for a commercial firm in order that the public may know of its existence and of the varied services that it offers."

OBJECTIVES OF PUBLIC RELATIONS: The main objectives of library public relation programmes are:

a. To create library consciousness among the people of the community.
b. To spotlight the existence of libraries where they are located, what do they contain, and to identify the services they can render to help people in their informal self-education.
c. To enrich and develop the subjects on which individuals are taking formal education.
d. To make constructive use of their leisure hours.
e. To become good citizens.
f. To help people remain well-informed.
g. To appreciate the values of democracy.

h.   To increase their theoretical knowledge.

Library public relation includesongoing activities to ensure that the library has a strong public image. Public relation is a management function of continuing and planned character through which public and private library seeks to win and retain the understanding, sympathy and support of those whom they are or may be concerned.

LIBRARY PUBLIC RELATIONS: A library public relations is deliberate, planned and sustained the effort to establish and maintain mutual understanding between the library and the public users. Relation activities help to provide a coordinated effort to communicate a positive image of the library and promote the availability of the library's material programme and services. The importance of public relation activities cannot be overlooked in any library, especially in academic libraries. The significance of academic libraries, specifically university libraries,cannot be overemphasized. University Library assists the university in the discharge of its functions by acquiring all relevant information necessary for teaching, learning, research and public services of the universities. This is to say that the objectives of any academic institution cannot be achieved without the presence of public relations. Any library activity, directly or indirectly, is an act of public relation in as much as it is done to promote the library image and its use.

ROLE OF REFERENCE LIBRARIAN: The reference librarian has the role of public relation office for the library. He goes outside the confines of thelibrary to carve a good image of the library in the minds of the potential users.A good number of libraries, especially academic libraries, offer so many commercial services unknown to users. It is the duty of reference librarian to inform the public about these services. The reference librarian may use handbills to pass on information to people and advertise library services.

The reference librarian is a part of the overall professional working to bring the desire to fulfilment. He has a lot to contribute to making the services of the library a success. A reference librarian can be referredto as the Public Relations Office of any library. He is the image booster to the library. He is doing his duties,which deal directly with the users. He is the intermediary between the users and the library. He can easily know what the users need and what the library has.

A librarian is the image-maker of the library. The Public Relations Officer in an organization is the image-maker and image-bearer of such an organization and, therefore, has many roles to play in order to ensure a good image forthe organization. This will involve their relationship with those who deal with the organization. The reference librarians are the image-makers, and indeed, the gateway through which people get in contact with the information of the library.

The reference librarian deals with isolated activities so as to bring them together, just like the Public Relations Officer of the organization. He acts as an intermediary between the users and the library resources, making them available to users. The Public Relations Officer tries to blow his organization's trumpet through the provision of information. The reference library disseminates the already acquired information to serve the users. He is a link between the library and the outside world to make known the activities of the library.

The public relations work is the administrative work concerned with the library which performs the undermentioned functions:

   i.   Assessment of ideas and opinion of the people.
  ii.   Framingthe policy and working method.
 iii.   To win the confidence ofthe people.

J.H. Right and B. H. Christian have defined the public relations in these words:"The present public contact is a well-planned programme of policies and behaviour aiming at increasing the knowledge and confidence in the people." In this way, it can be said that public contact is a well-planned programme of working policies and behaviour. The library officials utilize this programme in fulfilling the below-mentioned purposes:

a. To make people enable good use of the study material.
b. To get them acquainted withthelibrary and encourage the book reading.
c. To acknowledge readers about new arrivals in the library.

All the above public relations works are done on the library campus. Hence, these works are called public relations works. The librarians go out of the library campus and make friendly relations with the community. They arrange for such programmes as all the residents of the adjacent area may be acquainted with the library.

OBJECTIVES OF REFERENCE LIBRARIAN: The first and foremost objective of the librarian is to keep the safety of the books. The second objective is to provide the public with library services to visitors. He endeavours to make his library popular among the masses. Public contact work helps him attain his objectives. The librarian is the powerful medium of creating interest in the readers about the library. He plays an active role in providing masses with the knowledge they need.

Work outside Library Campus:There are several other public relations works. They are as such:

a. To publish new arrivals in the newspaper.
b. To collect data of published books.
c. To publish necessary information about the functions, gathering, meetings, seminars, etc.
d. To arrange for lectures from time to time on the public places to give knowledge about the library services to the public.
e. Circulation of handbills, pamphlets, leaflets, etc. among the masses.

f. Library staffto visit the houses in their respective areas and establishing personal contacts with them.

g. To stick posters on the walls, to display cinema slides in the local cinema halls.

h. Arranging conversation on radio and television over library activities andbooks collection.

i. To publish an annual report of the library and to distribute it in public.

The Need forPublic Relations Services: The demand for books or thirst for knowledge is momentary. If this thirst is not quenched in time, it dies soon. The process of study is a life-long process. Public libraries are run by the finance collected from the public. Hence, it is essential that the public should be aware of the number of books and the number of members and similar other data. The books can neither speak for them nor show their utility. Publicity is essential to displayits utility and importance. The basis of the progress of the library is successful public contact programmes. If the public is satisfied with the services rendered by the library,an increase in its income is always ascertained. A common man is not acquainted with the various activities and services of the public library. Hence, public relations is the most useful medium to make them well acquainted with the library and its various kinds of services.

CHAPTER 27

LIBRARY EXTENSION SERVICES

The extension services are an effort of a library to increase the number of its users to make the maximum use of its resources. It is an effort to inform the public about its resources, services and utility.

As a social animal, we have relations with our family members, relatives, neighbours, colleagues, etc. We make all effort to improve the relation and to do our best to prove the usefulness of relations with them. We also extend our sphere of relations by making new relations. Similarly, an institution keeps a relation with its customers, suppliers, investors, etc. It is necessary asapart of any organization which runs with public funds and for public services. Likewise, a library that is a social institution also keeps relation with users whom it gives services and other libraries whose resources are used by it.

Extension services are those works through which library message reads those persons who are unaware of the services rendered by the library. By performing this function,the library serves the maximum number of people in the society, and thus fulfils its liability. The main objective of the library is to make available to the maximum number of people the benefits of the library services and to attract more and more readers towards it. We can define extension service saying that it is to make the services reach the readers and make the maximum use of study material.

OBJECTIVES: The library extension service arouses aptitude for studying the study material available in the library. The main objectives of library extension services are as under:

a. It creates and stimulates the desire for good reading and brings books and readers together.
b. It makes maximum use of library resources.
c. It is to create an image of the library among the public and the

government.

d. To give information about the use of the library.

e. To attract towards the library services, those persons who are unable to use library services.

f. To make the people, who are making the use of the library, acquainted well with the library services so that they may make its maximumuse.

g. To make the library services effective.

h. To make acquainted with the reading material of the library.

i. To make all the persons, who are or are not the readers, familiar with the study material and services available in the library.

j. To render help in the eradication of illiteracy and ignorance.

k. It is an attempt to turn the library into a social centre which encourages reading.

FACETS: To perform the extension services effectively, the following facets in terms of infrastructure, equipment, skilled staff, etc. are needed:

a. To execute any extension service, proper planning by considering all the concerned aspects is necessary. Inadequacy at any part may fail the whole programmes.

b. All the extension services must be to encourage the people to use the library and to make the maximum utilization of library resourcesforthe development of the society.

c. The library should have a lecture hall, an exhibition lobby, conference room, etc. To organize a workshop, lectures, debates exhibitions, music concerts and other social and cultural programmes.

d. The library should have a multimedia projector, audio-visual elements like slide and film projector, mike, recording facility,etc.

e. The librarian and other library staff should be able to establish good public relations in the community so that maximum community members may participate in such programmesactively.

f. The coordination and cooperation among the staff members is also an important element for the successful execution of extension services.

To conclude, the main objective of extension services is to create interest in the readers towards the library through various extension techniques.

CHAPTER 28

FUNCTIONS OF ACQUISITION SECTION

The objective of the acquisition section is to make available the great literature to the maximum number of readers for the minimum funds. Main objectives of this section are as under:

a. To make education and knowledge available to all.
b. To lead people on the path of duty for the welfare of the nation and abroad.
c. To make books available to the deserving readers.
d. Tomaintain and accelerate the work of scientists, scholars and researchers.
e. To keep up the flow of the stream of knowledge.

Procurement of Books: In the acquisition cell, the books are acquired for the library. After the acquisition of the books, the following process is completed:

i. Book Order: To appoint a book supplier and to issue purchase orders.
ii. Supply: When books are supplied, the librarian compareswiththeorder and makes an endorsement on it.

Book Order: Action is taken for the procurement of the books in the library. The books are chosen after great consideration. Books are supplied in the library in three ways:

I. Books received a donation.
II. Books received in exchange.
III. Books purchased.

In fact, a few books are received in the donation and in exchange. Most of the books are purchased on the basis of the price list.At the beginning of the financial year, the librarian calls for the price lists from locals as well as from other cities. Thereafter, a comparative study is made of the pricelists. The bookseller, whose price list is found proper, useful, favourable and the lowest one, is appointed as the supplier of the book for that financial year.

In most of the libraries, the librarians invite quotations for the supply of the books. These quotations are invited from the bookseller in the city and out of the city. Aproforma is forwarded to the bookseller inviting quotations. The terms and conditions for the supply of books should be clearly specified.

After the appointment, the supplier is placed with the order for books. Often in the order, the books are mentioned under various subjects. The books are serialized according to the names of their authors alphabetically. Full particulars about the books are furnished.

Generally, three copies of the order are prepared. The original copy is forwarded to the supplier. The second copy is forwarded to the Head of the Department or the concerned officer. The third copy of the order is placed in the office file. If the number of books is greater, a list of the books is attached to the order.

The books should be sent according to the order and not their substitutes. If books sent by the supplier are found different from those mentioned in the order or defective in any way or incomplete and damaged, they will be returned to him at his expenses. The amount of the said books will be deducted from the bill, and the remaining amount will be passed for payment.

Do send only the latest edition of the books as far as possible. The books sent through VPP will not be accepted. If it is essential to send the books through the mail, do send by registered post. The price published abroad should be in original and thereafter transformed into country currency. Order No. and date should be endorsed on the bill invariably. The bill should be in good handwriting or typed.

Send books through road transport. Send the ability through the bank.Send only one copy of each book unless ordered otherwise. Responsibility of getting the books delivered in the library is of the supplier.In case books are not received in due time, the order would stand cancelled. Damage, if any, to the parcel, the loss will be borne by the supplier.

Publisher price should be mentioned in the bill. Discount is to be allowed on each book as per rates approved by the librarian. Keep a copy of the Bill in the packet of the books sent by road transport. The following precautions are to be observed before placing an order:

Before placing the order, it should be verified if the ordered books are not already present in the library. In that position, there is a possibility of the purchase of unnecessary books. The reason is that some of the ordered books may be already present in the library. Hence, the librarian should try to avoid unnecessary repetition. According to Dr Vibhasi, the librarian should verify the books catalogue, permanent order cards, pending orders, books received under orders, lying in the process of acquisition or classification or cataloguing. If it is verified that some of the books included in the order are already available in the library, such books are deleted from the order, and the remaining books are ordered.

The receipt department receives books. The booksellers oftencome in person and supply the books. The publishers and booksellers of other towns send their books through mail or railway or road transport. The books sent by mail are delivered in the library by the postman. Books sent by rail or road transport are to be collected by the library employee from the parcel office or transport company. The bookseller or publisher sends the railway receipt of the books to the company. The library should take prompt steps to get the delivery of the books as soon as they get the receipt. If any undue delay is made, the library has to pay the penalty to railway authorities. After the books have been received in person through railway or road transport, they are tallied with bill and got confirmed that all the books mentioned in the bill have been received in the library. Thereafter, books are arranged in the serial number, as mentioned in the bill.

After a close nomination, it is confirmed that every book is completely faultless. The books found faulty are returned to the bookseller at his responsibility and expenses. If thebooksellerfindshimself unable to send fresh books in exchange for the returned faulty books, he has to send credit note on the basis of it. The library makes the necessary deduction in the price of books before releasing the payment. The letter containing inconsistencies should be dispatched to the bookseller, publisher and supplier. Otherwise, there is a possibility of great loss to the library.

CHAPTER 29

ACCESSION REGISTER

A book may be received in the library through purchase, donation or received under copyright. The details of the books received in the library are entered in the Acquisition Register data-wise. This register is also called an Accession Register. It is a permanent record. Hence, it is essential that the paper used in this register should be of fine quality. It's binding also should be fine and strong. There are so many columns on both pages left and right. A standard Acquisition Register should have the following columns:

Date of Accession: In this column has entered the date on which the particulars of the acquired books are entered. This column reflects the development period of the books in the library.

Accession Number: In this column, the number of the book is entered. The number highlights how the library has gone prosperous. If certain books are not traceable in the library, the full particulars about the books are made available under this column.

Author's Name: In this column, the name of the author of the book as printed on its title page is entered.

Title: In this column are entered the particulars of the book title. If *A, An* or *The* is at the beginning of the title, these words are left. The only pure title is written. Sometimes the title of the books may belong.Hence, they need a long space. In such cases, the first one ortwo words and the last word are written. Between them,"dots" are used.Suppose, there is a book titled "A Handbook of International Study in South Asia", the title of this book would be entered like this- "Handbook... Asia."

Year of Publication: Every book must mention the year of publication. In this column, the year in which the book is published and out is entered. Some books have the mentioning of the month also alongwith the year of publication. In such circumstances, the month alongwith year should be entered.

Edition: If the book is published for more than one edition, the number of edition is entered here.

VolumeNumber: If there is more than one volume of the book, the number of the volume is entered in this column.

Place and Name of the Publisher: The book's title page must have the name of the publisher and his address. This information is entered in the Acquisition Register. It is written like this: New Delhi, Rupa Publication.

Pages: Number of the pages is given in this column. If the book is divided into many parts and page number in each part starts afresh, the total number ofpagesin each part is entered separately in this column.

Source of Receipt: The books may be purchased from the same bookseller, or it might be gifted from some other person or institution. The name and full particulars of thebooksellerare entered.

Bill Number and Date: The booksellers send the bill for the release of the payment. The serial number and date are given on that bill. The bill number and date are entered in this column.

Real Price of the Book: In this column, the printed price of the book is entered. The price of foreign publications also is entered in the same currency as is mentioned in the book. For example,$200.

Book Number: Every book is givena book number in the library. It helps the librarian to issue the book to the readers. It also helps to verify the stock as and when required.

Withdrawal Number and Date: Sometimes the books become unserviceable after long use, on being lost, pagesaretorn, pages removed or after when they becomeoutdated. In these circumstances, the books are removed from the library. The books removed from the library are identified, and their full particulars are entered in another register. This register is called Withdrawal Register. In this register, similar to the

Acquisition Register, there is a column for number and date which bears the full particulars of the book withdrawn.

Remarks: If the librarian has some more information to note in the Accession Register in addition to the information given in the various columns, there is a separate remarks column.

Need for Accession Register: We need the Accession Register for the following reasons:

a. Chronological order: We need the register to fix and find out the chronological order of any particular book among the other books collected in the library.

b. To mention the library property: In this register, the full particulars of a book and the number allotted to it are entered. By adopting this process, it is declared that the book is a library property.

c. Permanent Stock: The Accession Register is a permanent record of the whole stock of books and other study material. For the audit purpose, this register is considered to be the most authentic.

d. Record of library collection: Details of books available in the library on any particular date and the number of books purchased or received from any other sources on any particular date are entered here. The above details are given in this register in chronological order. This record register furnishes full bibliographical particulars about a book in the library. This book is indispensable to get the particulars about a book.

e. The Acquisition Register provides information about a book right from its acquisition in the library to its withdrawal. This register provides us with the utmost information.The last accession number reflects the prosperity of the library. It keeps us informed about the gradual and chronological development of the books in the library.

f. The register keeps us informed about the gradual and chronological development of the books in the library.

g. Stock Verification: In case, shelf-list is not available or maintained in the library, this register serves as the stock verification register. By endorsing the accession serial number on the bill, it is verified that the books mentioned in the above bill have been received in the library and payment in respect of them can be made.

h. Record for physical verification: In case of poor maintenance or non-availability of the shelf-list, this register is used for physical verification.

i. If the books are destroyed due to an outbreak of fire or any other natural calamity, the insurance company compensates on the basis of the Accession Register.

CHAPTER 30

LIBRARY BOOK NUMBER

There is a huge collection of books, manuscripts, literature and scholarly papers on different subjects in a library. It becomes difficult to arrange the books in order. In order to solve this problem, one subject is provided with a uniform number. The arrangement of book number is made for placement of the books in order. The characteristic of a book is shown in this way- title of the book, author's name, language of the book, yearof publication, edition and its volume.

The book number is the accession number of the book. Book number provides personality to a book. The arrangement of a book should be made in a scheme of classification so that the books related to one subject can be arranged together in a mechanized way.

Creating Book Number: There is a system to create abooknumber. In every system, the different virtues of the book are used as under:

    a. On the basis of the surname of the author,
    b. On the basis of the title of the book, and
    c. On the basis of publication of the year.

According to this system, the three letters of the surname of the author are used to form a book number. Or, the name of the author is translated into digits for creating a book number. Also, we can use the year of publication as the base for book number. In order to create a book number, there is a provision of time series. The document which was published earlier is put first and the second one is put next.

CHAPTER 31

INTERNATIONAL STANDARD BOOK NUMBER

The International Standard Book Number (ISBN) is a numeric commercial Book identifier which is intended to be unique. Publishers purchase ISBN from an affiliate of the International ISBN Agency.An ISBN is assigned to each edition and variation of a book. ISBNs were ten digits in length to the end of December 2006. But since 1 January 2007, theyconsist of 13 digits. ISBNs are circulated using a specific mathematical formula andinclude a check digit to validate the number. Each ISBN consists of 5 elements with each section being separated by spaces or hyphens. These elements are:

Primary Element: Currently, this can only be either 978 or 979. It is always 3 digits in length.

Registration Group Element:This identifies the particular country, geographical region, language, and are participating in the ISBN system. This element may be between 1 and 5 digits in length.

Registrant Element: This identifies the particular publisher or imprint. This may be up to 7 digits in length.

Publication Element: This identifies the particular edition and format of the specific title. This may be up to six digits in length.

Check Digit: This is always the final and single digit that mathematically validates. The rest of the number is calculated using a Modulus 10 system with alternate weightsof 1 and 3.

What is an ISBN for? An ISBN is essentially a product identifier used for publishers, booksellers, libraries, internets, retailer and other supply chain participants for listing, sales, records and stock control purpose. The ISBN identifies the registrant as well as the specific title, edition and format.

What does an ISBN identify? ISBN is assigned to tax-based monographic publication,i.e. one of the publications rather than journals,newspapers, or other types of serials. Any book made publically available for sale can be identified by the ISBN. In addition, individual sections such as chapters of a book,articles,journals or periodicals that are made available separately may also use the ISBN as an identifier.

With regard to the various media available, it is of no importance in what form the content is documented and distributed. However, different products, e.g. paperback, epub, pdf, should be identified separately. The ISBN is an identifier and does not convey any form of legal or copyright protection.

Who should apply for ISBN? It is always the publisher of the book who should apply for the ISBN. For the purpose of ISBN, a publisher is a group, company and individual who is responsible for initiating the production of a publication. Normally, it is also the person or body who bear the cost and the financial risk in making a product available. It is not normally the printer, but it can be the author of the book if the author has chosen to publish their book themselves.

CHAPTER 32

CATALOGUING

Meaning and Definition: Library catalogue means the list of books and documents available in a library. According to James Duff Brown, "Catalogue is explanatory, logically arranged inventory and key to the books." Charles Amni opines, "A catalogue is a list of books which is arranged on some definite plan." It is a list of books in some library or collection. Dr S. R. Ranganathan says, "Catalogue is a list of books and documents in a library or in a collection forming a portion of it." Dr M. S. Swaminathan opines, "It is a tool which gives information about the contents of the library. It is divided into two parts- the subject and the author. It gives information about the arrangement in which they are lying on the shelves. It helps the reader to find out his desired book without any loss of time. It saves the time of the reader and the staff."

It is evident from the above that the library catalogue is an absolute and arranged list of reading material available in a library. It gives the information about the location of each book and other reading material on the shelves by which these can be found without wasting time.

A library has a huge amount of books. It is difficult to differentiate one from the other. Hence, in order to access a particular book easily, cataloguing of the books and classification thereof is necessary. By classification, the displayof the books on the shelves isdetermined. Through classification, the books can be kept physically in one place. It is only cataloguing that makes the readers reach the desired books through various ways, e.g. author, title, series, edition, topic, etc.

Cataloguing is done after classification.The reason is that the subject heading is determined by the classification. It saves the labour and time of the cataloguer. It is essential for the cataloguer to keep the catalogue up to date. It will enable the readers to have correct information about the books available in the library. Otherwise, readers would have to waste their time in search of books.

Cataloguing Process: The technical department does the work of cataloguing for arranging the study material collected in the library. Thereafter, a catalogue is prepared to give information about the study material tothe reader. The various works are done under the cataloguing process,such as to determine the entries, to make the entries, to examine the entries, to arrange the entries and to maintain the brief description of these steps.

After determining the number of the entries, the cataloguer makes the entries on the basis of the catalogue code recognised by the library. The entries are written on the card. Often senior trained cataloguer makes the main entry with a pencil. A junior staff member makes its copy on the card either with hand or with type machine. Then, the entries are kept in the book.

After making the entries according to rule, they are to be kept in a helpful and logical sequence for the users. The form of the modern catalogues is cards. Only one entry can be made on each card. Complete and corrected entries are arranged on their proper place in the catalogue. The library does this work on the basis of the predetermined technique.The entries are arranged word by word; letter by letter.

Objectives of Library Catalogue: The chief objective or aim of the library catalogue is providing accurate directions to the readers concerning the reading material required by them. It aims at enabling each and every reader to get the reading material required by him easily at the earliest. It aims at saving his time. The reader goes through it and comes to know about the reading material on the shelves. Thus, he finds the required reading material without loss of time. The main objectiveis to enable a reader to get the book needed by him.The library catalogue aims at providing information to the visitors about the books available in the library. The catalogue provides information on various books written by a particular author available in the library. It also aims at assisting the readers in the selection of the books available in the library.

DrS.R.Ranganathanhas given some suggestions about the formation of the catalogue. According to him, the catalogue should be formed in such a manner as it may serve the following objectives:

a. Enabling every reader to obtain the book desired or needed by him.
b. Enabling every book to reach its appropriate reader.
c. Minimising the wastage of the reader's time.
d. Minimising the wastage of the library staff's time.

I.G. Mudge also has expressed his views on the objectives of the library catalogue. He treats it as a tool meant for providing correct or accurate information on the undermentioned different points to readers. The catalogue shows if any specific book on the headingofwhich the reader has information is available in the library.

It also gives a description of the bibliographical facts about those books which are generally required or needed by common readers. It provides an exhaustive list complete in all respect of the books, booklet, or reading material written or published in any form by a particular author. An exhaustive list of published material on a specific subject is always available in the library. Dr Vibhasi has described the main purposes of library catalogue as under:

1. The library catalogue provides to the visiting readers required information about the complete reading material or a part of it available in the library.
2. It provides information about the availability of books as well as its location. To provide information under the various headings to the user, if the book required by him is available in the library or not. In case it is available, what exact its location

is!

3. Providing information about the status of the reading material. The catalogue provides the readers or visitorswiththe subject-wise information about the status of books and other reading material that is available in the library.

CHAPTER 33

IMPORTANCE OF LIBRARY CATALOGUE

The various functions performed by the library catalogue exhibit that it is important tool equipment for any library. The bigger the library is, the more its importance is. Its importance becomes manifold in a Public Library and a University Library where the reading material is in large number. The functioning of a library without a catalogue cannot be imagined. The importance of library catalogue can be described as under:

a. It is upon the quality of a library's catalogue that the maximum use of the reading materials collected therein depends.

b. A comprehensive, accurate, complete, up to date and exhaustive catalogue enhances the desire of the library.

c. A comprehensive and accurate catalogue assists in enhancing the use of the library by the readers in a greater number.

d. A comprehensive catalogue is of great use in providing complete information about the needed books to the readers.

e. A comprehensive catalogue serves as a coordinator between the needs of the readers and the reading material available in the library.

f. The library catalogue provides the readers with the complete description of the multifocal reading material, including books concerning more than one subject.

In the library, the books are arranged in the shelves in accordance withthe microscopic classification of a specific subject. In such an hour of necessity, catalogue comes for their help. Sometimes one and the same book is concerned with two or more subjects. For example, the books of Political Science and Sociology. Now, this book can be placed only on one shelf either in the Political Science Department or on the Sociology Department. In case, it is kept in the Political Science Department; the readers making the search for it in the Sociology Department would not be able to trace it, get it and make use of it. In such a moment, catalogue proves to be of great importance.

The library is visited by serious readers and researchers also.They get complete information about the subject. The form of the library makes no difference to them. In other words, it bears no importance for them, if the information needed by them is available in a complete book or in a part of some book or in some periodical.Such serious students are bound to ransack all the books if a catalogue is not available to guide them.

There are some readers who might be acquainted with the titles of the books or at most of their author's name. They demand the books quoting these names. Their demand can be met with by the library catalogue only. Otherwise, it is not practicable for them to make a search for them among the books scattered on various shelves. The catalogue provides useful information about the book if it is already issued to some reader or is available in the library. It becomes more useful if it is printed and made available to the visitors for reference. To sum up, cataloguing is of great importance as such:

a. It facilitates proper utilization of readingthematerial in the library.
b. It increases the number of readers.
c. It adds to the popularity of the library.
d. It enables the library to attain its objectives.

NECESSITY OF CATALOGUING: A library is evaluated by the availability of the useful reading material in the library, and not by its spacious building, qualification of the librarian and the staff, etc.

Cataloguing of the reading material is essential to make it useful. It is of such vital importance that it is called the key to the library. In the absence of a catalogue,thelibrary will not be able to function properly and would be no better than a city without light. In a dark city, a traveller is bound to stumble and fail in reaching his destination. In the same way, in the absence of catalogue, the reader would not be able to reach his needed book. Too much time of the visitor would be wasted in reaching the book.Even the staff members would have to waste a lot of time in finding out the books needed. It is quite evident that the time if saved, could have been utilized in useful tasks.The catalogue enables the library staff to find out the needed book without wastage of time.

A well organized, accurate, elaborate, exhaustive and up-to-date catalogue, complete in every respect, enhances the prestige and utility of a library.The staff providing the reference service will also be grouping in the dark and hence fail to perform his task. Instead of guiding, he will simply misguide the readers in view of the incomplete and inaccurate catalogue. The use of the library will be adversely affected bytheabsence of a catalogue. When the readers fail to get the needed reading material, they will discontinue their coming.

CHAPTER 34

BOOK CIRCULATION

A big library has a vast number of books and other reading material. Also, there are a number of readers enrolled in the library. In the interest of the readers, there are frequent activities of the issue and receipt of books and other literary items. The process through which a reader is allowed to take the books out of the library for reading is called Issue System. The whole process through which the library gets back the books is called Return System.

Library circulation comprises the activities around the lending of books and other materials to users of the library. It provides lending facilities forthereturn of loaned items. Renewal of materials and payment of fines are handled at the circulation desk.

A circulation or lending department is one of the key departments of a library. The main public service point is the circulation desk usually found near the main entrance of a library. It provides lending services and facilities forthereturn of loaned items. Renewal of material and payment of times are also handled at the circulation desk. Circulation staff may provide search and reference services. The circulation desk is, in most cases, staffed by library support staff instead of professional librarians.Functions of circulation desk staff are mentioned below:

    a. Lending materials to library users.
    b. Checking in materials returned.
    c. Monitoring materials for damage or routing them to the appropriate staff for repair or replacement.
    d. Charging and receiving overdue fines.
    e. Sent out overdue notices to borrower.
    f. Operating automated filling and recording system.
    g. External communication and interpersonal skills.
    h. Adapt to new software and equipment.

i.   Ability toreconcile financial resources.
j.   Communication via telephone, email.
k.   Ability to see and read the material.
l.   Assist patrons at the circulation desk.
m.   Assist circulation supervisor in trainingofstudentsandemployees.
n.   Resolve issues such as inappropriate patron conduct, including but not limited to cellphone users, open drink containers and inappropriate noise levels.

A library is successful if the study material collected in that library is utilized more and more. For its maximum utilization,anumber of the readers is possible only in the condition that the study material is available to the readers, and they are allowed to utilize the study material outside the library also.The libraries provide such facilities through the book circulation system. At present, nearly all the libraries provide their readers with such facilities.

In the present days, the publication is an unlimited number. Hence, the circulation system in the library has become significant. This function has become essential in view of abiding by the laws of library science. The libraries fulfil the needs of such readers through the book circulation system.

CHAPTER 35

REFERENCE SECTION

In the term of library science, the reference section is the section that provides literary reference services to the readers. It is established in almost all libraries. Keeping in view its importance of imparting significant knowledge on different subjects, it is called the heart of the library. In the absence of its services, a reader is likely to be lost in the library. He would have to waste much of his time searching for reading material.

The reference section provides the readers with reference services. They approach the reference section to get specific information or detailed information on a subject. In this way, his precious time and labour are saved. A reference section is needed in the library for the following reasons:

i. The readers need personal assistance to enable them to understand the utility of the subject matter and the proper method of using it.

ii. The text of so many books is sometimes presented in a typical manner. As a result, the readers face problem in the section in the use of these books. They need some personal assistance to enable them to understand the utility ofthe subject matter andto find out the proper methodof using the subject matter of the book. The required assistance is provided by the reference section.

iii. The extensive use of library facilitates the readers to understand the basic rules of cataloguing. This work is done in the reference section. The reference section introduces the readers to the basic rules likesbook selection, book order, contemporary publication, classification and cataloguing of books, accession of books, distribution of books, display, exhibition and circulation of books, etc.

We need the services of a reference section to arouse and maintain interest for the library in the visiting readers. It is essential to provide them with the material of their interest. This work is to be done at the earliest as soon as the readers visit the library.

If the visiting readers are not provided with the above material, they may lose interest. Consequently, they may be discouraged from visiting the library. It is the task of the reference section to provide the visiting readers with such services to enable them to get the desired book in the least possible time.

In the present day world, there is a rapid increase in the growth and distribution of literature. Hence, it is essential to organize and decentralize the vast spread of literature. This task is undertaken by the Reference Section.

FUNCTIONS OF REFERENCE SECTION: Main functions of the reference section are mentioned below:

The Reference Section provides the readers with general guidance when it is required by them. The section brings into the notice of the visiting readers the various books, especially new arrivals in the library. It locates the books desired by the readers. It makes available to the readers the located books. It imparts training to the readers. It makes the best use of the reading material available in the library.

Since the number of publication has grown manifold, it is not possible for readers to go through all. Hence,there comes the reference staff for their aid. The Reference Section maintains up-to-date information regarding reference books. Itcompilesinformation on the reading material available in the library. It maintains indices and subject-wise catalogues of books.

To conclude, the reference section performs activities so that the visiting readers may make the maximum use of the reading material in the librar

CHAPTER 36

PERIODICAL SECTION

There is a vast importance of periodical section. Newspapers and magazines have their own importance. They maintain a good position in furnishing current knowledge to the readers.

Dr Vibhasimentions:"Periodical denotes a magazine which is published after regular intervals; say weekly, fortnightly, monthly or quarterly, containing articles, not by a single author but contributed by a number of authors."

Dr S. Ranganathan has defined magazines or periodicals like this:"Magazines or periodicals are those timely publications whose every volume is normally formed by independent, separate and personal contributions of two and more authors in which continuity of thought is absent, and the articles on specific subject and the contributions in its subsequent volumes are also different, but all the subject belongs to the same field of knowledge."

It is generally not published as a complete volume, but it is published in parts or issues. It inevitably spreads knowledge. Information in its everyvolume is not repeated by updating information in the same form.

It imparts the latest knowledge. The latest developments are comprised of in it. The articles incorporated in it are not written by one author but are contributed by more than one authors.The articles are not in continuation. It contains several thoughts. It is invaluable for those who are preparing for competitions or research work. A periodical undergoes the following stages before finding a place in a library. The various stages of the process are a periodical selection process, periodical ordering process, and periodical maintenance record.

The Selection Process: The selection of proper and useful periodicals is a tedious job. The reason is that there is a flush of periodicals and magazines in the market. The chief bases for selection of publications are the nature and scope of the library, the inclinations, demands and trends of the readers, the financial resources ofthelibrary, the periodicals available in other libraries, the burning issues, nagging problems, etc.

DrVibhasi suggests that coordination and natural discussions held amongst the library staff, readers, researchers and subject specialists serve as feedback and are of great importance. Their suggestions should be kept in view while selecting the periodicals.

Generally, there is no discount on the purchase of periodical. However, some agents tend to give for a fixed period in their own way. In case no discount is offered, the annual subscription charges may be given to the agents or representatives of the publisher.

In case the publisher agrees to the term and conditions of the library, standing order can be given forthe whole year. The subscription for the purchase of periodicals is always sent for the year, not for each periodical.

The periodicals may be purchased from a local seller or representative. Althoughit is a bit more expensive, yet it is a convenient process. The process of acquiring periodicals through the various stages is as under:

First of all, approval of the concerned officials for the purchase of the periodicals is obtained. Thereafter, complying with the whole purchasing rules, orders are sent, and procurement is made.

CHAPTER 37

BOOK MAINTENANCE SECTION

Harry MillerLadenberg and John Archer have held in their book "The Care And Repair Of Books" that the books are like children as an answer to the care and concern during the initial stages of life and as an answer to the environment and family traditions.

It is evident from the above that there are a great number of similarities between books and children on the one hand and the library staff and parents on the other. The parents protect their infants against any injury or mishappening and wish them a happy life. In the same way, the library staff protects the books against any damage and wish them a long life.

Functions: The function of taking care of the books is performed by the maintenance section of the library. To take care of the books, to save the books against any possible damage and to repair the books,if damaged, are the main functions of the book maintenance section. To verify and rectify the books from time to time is its chief function. The various functions performed by the maintenance section are as under:

The library staffarranges the books in order of classification.This is the first and foremost function of the maintenance section. The books should be arranged in order of classification so that they may be immediately found in their proper place when a reader looks up.

In the open shelf or open access system, the readers go to the racks and select the books personally. There is all possibility of their misplacing the books in a hurry or without giving a thought to their actions. In such a situation, the other readers who wish to read those books may not find the books as they will look up only in their proper or original places. In such a position, the staff of the maintenance section should make a thorough checking of the books in the different cupboard and racks regularly. They should ensure that the books are kept in their original places in the cupboard.

The books are to be protected against the damage caused to them at various hands. It is observed that the books are damaged at three hands as under:

    a. Damage caused by library staff,
    b. Damage caused by readers, and
    c. Damage caused by Nature.

As soon as the books are received in the library, it becomes the responsibility of the librarian to take due care of them. Before the books are given to the readers, the books pass through many hands. Now, the librarian and the staff membersareexpectedto take care of the books, as if these were their personal property. In practice, it is seen that the librarian instructs the staff members to take care of the books properly. In case the librarian or other staff members are not careful, the books are caused to damage knowingly or unknowingly.Thereare several causes of damage to books:

    I. Lack of Knowledge: The staff members lack the knowledge of the possible cause of damage to the books. They may be unaware oftheprecautionary step as well.

    II. Keeping the Books Carelessly: Sometimes books are dropped carelessly while they are to be kept and arranged in the shelves. As a result, titles and pages are torn. Sometimes books are not keeping straight in the shelves. Instead, they remainto bend to one side. Such books are disfigured. Books are damaged, if there are no book supporters in the racks.

    III. Carelessness and Recklessness: When the book parcels are received and opened, carelessness and recklessness at the end of the library,staffdamagethe books when they are opened.

    IV. Marking on Page: Sometimes the damage is caused to the

books as the names of ownership are marked onpagesofthe books.

V. RoughHandling: There is the rough handling of thebooks,which causes damage to them. Rough handling may be as under:

a. There is rough handling when the books are delivered from one place to the other. Books are sometimes thrown out to pass them over.

b. Books are put down roughly when these are received in the circulation section.

c. The books may fall on the floor.

d. The books may be bent.

e. The books may be curved.

f. The books may be torn or disfigured.

Preventive Steps: To avoid damage that may be caused to the books by the librarian or library staff, the following preventive measures should be taken:

I. Only capable and responsible persons should be appointed in the library. If some staff members behaveirresponsibly,they may be taken to task and suitable orders to be given to them to behave well and do properly.

II. The staff members should be kept under strict supervision. It should be watched minutely and ensured that no one is mishandling with the books.

III. The books should not be placed too high in the racks. The height should be reachable.

IV. The stamp of ownership should be carefully marked on the correct page of the book to avoid disfiguring it.

CarefulHandling: Books should be carefully carried and delivered from one place to another place in the library or from one library toanother library. The books should neither be thrown down nor dropped but carefully placed. It should not be kept in the wronglocation. Avoid disfiguring the books with touching. The books should not be touchéd with dirty or wet hands. The books should be sent for repair and rebinding as the case may be,andnodelay should be made in taking this step. If the damaged books are not repaired, they will go from bad to worse. They should be pulled out from the shelves properly and carefully. They should be placed straight in the shelves. There should be regular cleaning of the shelves. Insecticides should be sprayed off and on. Measures should be taken so that ants should not spoil the books.

Damage Caused by the Reader: Some indisciplined, ill-witted or anti-social elements cause damage to the books. This type of behaviour is seen in almost every library. Some readers cause damage for their no avail. Following kinds of damages to the books are caused by the readers:

Some readers use force while deriving or taking out the books from the shelves. While they do so, the spine of the books is damaged. The binding also is broken. Sometimes as they are asleep, the books fall on the floor, and their binding is broken, or pages are torn. Thus, books are disfigured.Sometimes the readers do not keep the books in a safe place at home. The place is reachable to the children. They take out the tag, date slip or book packet.

Some readers spoil the books. They mark underlines; they write some notes and useless comments. They often keepapen or pencil in the book. This weakens the binding of the book. Sometimes the readers keep a pen or pencil inside the book so that they may resume its reading from the page on the next day. But due to this act, the binding of the books is broken. Sometimes the readers, while reading the book, bend or fold the pages of the book. This act spoils the book.

Taking off pages, photos, pictures are very bad habits of some disturbing readers. They tear off the pages containing important or attractive photos, pictures, diagrams, charts, tables, etc. This act causes loss to other readers as they are deprived of the matter given on that page as well as overleaf.

Sometimes attractive, costly and important magazines are stolen by the miscreants. This act causes a great loss to the library. Sometimes such magazines have been procured from abroad and hence; it becomes almost impossible to replace them. There is a misuse of open shelf facility. In the open shelf, readers mishandle books and leave them helter-skelter. This act causes inconvenience to the next readers.

Preventive Measures: Various preventive measures are suggested to reduce the above-mentioned types of damages. Some areas under:

To create awareness: The awareness of the fact that the books in the library are public property should be inculcated in the readers. In every member of society,a sense of responsibility should be created. The readers should realize it to be of their own responsibility to take care of these books. Conducting awareness of programme should be there from time to time. In these programmes, the readers should be made acquainted with the proper method of handling and using the books of the library.

The readers should be made aware of their duties and responsibilities towards the library though printed pamphlets, booklets and brochures. When the books are returned by the readers to the library, they should be carefully checked. The readers who have caused any damage to the books should be awarded punishment like temporary expulsion, fine, etc. Legal action may be taken in extreme cases. The library staff should take regular care of the library premises and keep staff alert. Special attention should be given to specific books. Specific books are those which are rare and out of print. Since there is a greater possibility of their being stolen, special attention should be paid to those books. Those books may be kept under lock and key.

Other Safety Measures: Library building should be fireproof. The proper arrangement should be made for fire fighting equipment such as fire extinguishers, electronic fire alarms,etc. These should be checked from time to time. Smoking should be strictly prohibited in the library premises. Often match sticks thrown on the floor cause fire. Inflammable material or substance that catches fire such as petrol, diesel, gases, rags and useless papers, etc. should never be stored inside the library building. If essential, they may be kept in the store. Regular inspection should be carried of electrical wiring with a view to examine it of itsbeingdamaged. Mousetraps should be used in the library. The use of wooden furniture should be avoided in the library. It should be replaced by iron steel. If it is essential, only good quality wood should be used for the furniture. The wooden furniture must be cleaned and painted with varnish every year.

The adequate measure should be taken so that the humidity may not become too highin the library. The windows must be kept shut in the season. All the shelves are swept and cleaned. Kerosene and benzene should be sprayed. It would prevent the possibility of termite damage. A mixture of chloric acid and sodium chloride should be sprayed in the shelves. It would prevent the damage caused by crickets, silverfish, cockroach, etc. These preventive measures may be taken to protect the books from white ants and termites.

CHAPTER 38

REPAIR AND BINDING OF BOOKS

The success of a library lies in attracting a maximum number of readers. It would lead to maximum utilization of the books. Inspite of the maximum care taken in handling the books, the books are likely to lose their shape over long use. The binding of the books becomes loose. The pages of the books become dirty and soiled. The general appearance of the books becomes shabby, and the readers refrain from reading them. In fact, shabby and dirty books fail to attract readers. As such, proper steps are to be taken to give such old books in the library a new lease of life by rebinding. Rebinding gives a new look as well as life to such books. Librarian bears the ultimate responsibility of maintaining the books. Following points are to be kept in view while giving books for repairing:

For repairing and binding of books, it is necessary to appoint a capable and reliable binder. The librarian himself should specify the standard and type of the materials for binding such as paper, hardboard, leather, cloth, etc. He must, in person, check the books minutely. He should satisfy himself as under:

a. Whether the subject-wise list, title page, index, etc. are attached in the proper place in the book.

b. Whether the materials used for binding books are the same as specified by the library while appointing the binder.

c. Whether the stitching of the magazines, periodicals or books is as per the directions were given to binder.

d. Whether the writing and printing of the letters embossed or printed on the spine of the books are neat, clear and legible.

e. While trimming the pages of the books for binding, no text of the book should be cut.

f. The torn pages of the books are repaired by using glue, cello-tape, etc. and are readable.

g. The librarian should ensure that proper care of the tables, charts, maps, diagrams, etc. of the books have been taken while binding them.

Repair and binding of books on a regular basis are essential in libraries so that books may remain attractive and useful for readers.

CHAPTER 39

STOCK RECTIFICATION

Stock rectification is also an important work in a library. In any library, now and then, it becomes necessary to withdraw the books that are either lost or damaged and hence cannot be used in the library. Damaged books occupy the space in the library for nothing. This space can be used for new arrivals. Hence, the rectification of books is needed.

The librarystaff is expected to keep in their mind while withdrawing books from the library,thatthey must remaininthe library and the rest copies should be withdrawn. When new editions are made available and procured, the old editions should be withdrawn.Outdated books lose their value by the passage of time and subject matter and content become outdated. Such books should be withdrawn. Damaged ortorn books should be withdrawn.Books on life and history should be kept with special care. Historical books or books based on life such as autobiography, etc. should be discarded only when these are badly damaged or rendered useless.Bookson social science should be withdrawn only when findingquite useless.

Old editions should be replaced by the new ones. Books on literature should be withdrawn only when new editions are procured. Books on natural science should be upgraded by acquiring new editions. Action for withdrawing the older editions should be taken. Books having grown unpopular can be replaced. Damaged books should be replaced annually. Reference books that have grown outdated should be replaced after every five or ten years by new editions or other new books on the same subject. This action may be taken according to the nature and utility of the books.

CHAPTER 40

STOCK VERIFICATION

Various types of readers visit and make use of books in the library. This uses to cause damage to the books in many forms. Sometimes they are put in the wrong places while some other times took away. Hence, it is essential to know which books are actually available in the library from time to time. For this, the staff members or the employees of the library carry out a physical inspection of the collection of books in the library every year. This work is called stock verification, i.e. physical verification or checking of the books present in the library.

The work of stock verification is not so easy. Instead, it is a very significant as well as complicated and time-consuming task. It requires strenuous efforts on the part of the library staff. It should be carried out with utmost care and sincerity.

Purpose of Verification: Main purposes of verification of library books are as under:

a. To know the actual condition of various classes of books.
b. To know exactly the number of books available in the library.
c. To know how many and which books are lost, misplaced or not returned to the library by its readers.
d. To know the physical condition of the books in the library.
e. To increase the efficiency of the employees of the library to make them aware of their responsibility towards the books.

Merits of Stock Verification: Chief merit of the stock verification is that we get to know about the books that are actually available in the library. The verification is made from the Accession Register. We also get to know about the books that are damaged and hence no longer useful. The administrators and the officials of the library realize that some damage is bound to be caused if the books and the other reading material available in the library are used. As such, they can take necessary actions for minimizing that damage to or loss of books.

The policymakers of the library can decide whether the open access system should be continued or discontinued in the library. It may be discontinued if the books are missing from the library. The stock verification also makes the employees and members of the staff realize their negligence and irresponsibility. They take proper steps to improve it. Disciplinary action can be taken against negligent employees. The fear keeps them conscious of their duty. The employees of the library grow more aware and responsible for their duties. By stock,the verification library catalogue is updated and made reliable. The books that are reported to be useful and popular but lost or damaged completely can be purchased again and made available for use by the reader.

We take action to withdraw useless and obsolete books from the library. We make a purchase of new copies of popular and important books. We also take steps for glueing of new tags, book pocket, or date-slip. The stock verification completes the task of rectification. Often it so happens that the books considered being lost in the library are found lying elsewhere during the process of stock verification. The books placed in the wrong locations are again placed in the correct locations in the racks. Any mistake or omission made in the process of classification or cataloguing is detected and can be corrected. Stock room is fully swept. Shelves, racks and books become clean and free from any harmful insects.

REFERENCES

1. Library and Information Science- D. K. Pandey
2. Library Manual- S. R. Ranganathan
3. The Five Laws of Library Science-S.R. Ranganathan

4. Libraries(10 pillars of Library & Information Science)-NarendraDodiya

5. Library Management- C.K. Sharma,Kiran Singh

6. Library and Society- Rai Technology University, Bengaluru

7. Library Information and Society- Dr SumangalaJha

8. Colon Classification- S. R. Ranganathan

9. Classified Catalogue Code- S.R. Ranganathan

10. Classification and Communication- S.R. Ranganathan

11. LibraryBook Selection-S.R. Ranganathan

12. Philosophy of Library Classification-S. R. Ranganathan

13. Reference Service- S. R. Ranganathan

14. E-book in Library: A Practical Guide, edited by Kate Price and Virginia Havergal

15. Library and Information Sciences: Trends and Research- Chuanfu Chen